Hello and welcome to the *Guardian Football Weekly*'s first – and, let's be honest given how it's turned out, probably last – attempt at a book. It's been a right hassle to put together, despite the best efforts of Max, Barry, Producer Joel and everybody at Faber, which have at least ensured there aren't too many blank pages, so please don't complain to the bosses.

Growing up in the 1980s, a key part of my footballing education was the football annual. After an unfortunate early incident in which a hideous sweatshirt met with my legendary diplomatic skills, my Aunty Doris learned her lesson, and I could guarantee she'd get me the *Topical Times* every Christmas. One of the grandparents usually managed *Shoot!* as well. So think of this as a tribute to the spirit of those annuals, just with less Kevin Drinkell and more despair.

Obviously, I was delighted to be given the chance to fill another hundred-odd pages with analysis of football in Hungary in the 1930s, but unfortunately this is a book designed by committee, so a lot of that has been cut to make space for quizzes and jokes and anecdotes and 'fun'. Apparently, that's what the readers want.

Which is bad news if you're interested in why Törekvés were relegated in 1938, the life and career of Gyula Zsengellér or the improbable rise of Csepel, but good news if you want to hear about Barry's accident on the Munich U-Bahn, Basile Boli's musical career or listeners' vasectomies. I'm told they've left some of the Hungarian stuff in, so there should be something worthwhile somewhere.

The classic way of ending these editors' intros is to say that I hope you have as much fun reading it as we did putting it together – but frankly, if you don't have a million times more fun, you'll be asking for your money back. And nobody wants that.

JONATHAN WILSON
London, April 2023 (I know, but, honestly, these deadlines are worse than Jools Holland's *Hootenanny*)

CONTENTS

BLIND DATE

BARRY ON MAX

What were you hoping for?
With our then presenter James Richardson either off presenting *World's Strongest Man* or on his skiing holiday, I was looking forward to a relatively pun-free hour or two of fun, belittling, undermining and generally bullying our equivalent of a supply teacher.

First impressions?
That Max is much bigger than he looks on telly, which I suppose is unsurprising, considering my TV set is a forty-inch Panasonic. It being the first time I'd seen him in 'real life', it seemed odd that he was not holding a clipboard while trying to elicit conversation from the bass player of a terrible indie band.

Any awkward moments?
I think he was slightly taken aback when, during a lull in conversation, I asked him about what kind of shenanigans went on in the post-show *Soccer AM* green room. It turns out it isn't – or wasn't – the hotbed of drug-fuelled hedonism I thought it was.

Good table manners?
Excellent. Max insisted on buying everyone present what he calls 'a posh coffee' from the prohibitively expensive café adjacent to Guardian Towers.

Best thing about Max?
He lives 10,503 miles away.

Would you introduce him to your friends?
I have introduced him to several London-based friends, both parents and my big sister, and he has also met and had lunch with one of my aunts. Everyone finds him depressingly charming, but I think a night on the lash in Birr with my Irish pals would really test his mettle.

Describe Max in three words.
Pinko liberal snowflake.

What do you think he made of you?
I think he liked the cut of my jib, because when talkSPORT offered him a Sunday-morning radio show, he insisted, in the face of what I believe to have been considerable boardroom hostility, on having me as his sidekick. I found out later he had been particularly tickled by my query about the *Soccer AM* green room.

Did you go on somewhere?
He pedalled away on his bicycle, and I didn't think our paths would ever cross again. How wrong I was . . .

And . . . did you kiss?
No, but in well over a decade, we have hugged twice: one slightly forced and insincere embrace when Max left for Australia, and a genuinely warm one when we found out that we no longer had to work with a certain former cyclist and knight of the realm on the radio.

If you could change one thing about the recording, what would it be?
I would not have asked to hear the origin story of his microwave oven.

Marks out of 10?
9.

Would you meet again?
Despite not inviting me to his wedding, he has become the nearest thing I have to a life partner, insofar as we never have sex and speak to each other only when absolutely necessary. I guess I'm stuck with him until I find somebody better and trade up.

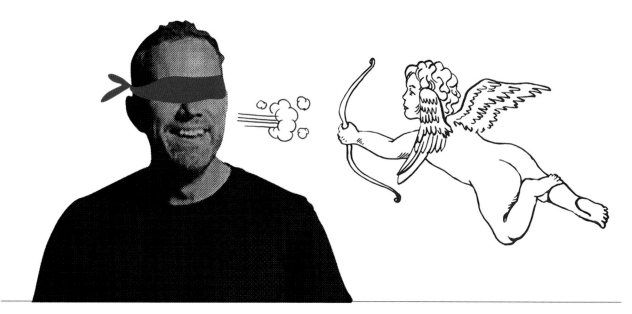

MAX ON BARRY

What were you hoping for?
Virtually zero expectations. I wasn't a pod listener the first time I covered for James Richardson. But this was the *Guardian*, the first time my snowflake leftie real friends would be proud of me and a world away from the laddy banter of *Soccer AM*. Finally, I could be the erudite, intellectual journalist I always aspired to be.

First impressions?
He looked like a *Guardian* journalist. He looked like a football journalist – withered, weathered, slightly fed up. But, all things considered, nothing special.

What did you talk about?
Well, we were just having a pleasant, if unspectacular, wander through whatever football had happened, until, about twenty minutes in, Barry asked me an incredibly inappropriate question involving nudity, cocaine and my personal carnal desires. This was not the kind of *Guardian* I was expecting. I was intrigued.

Any awkward moments?
He shat himself.

Good table manners?
Excellent. Although not on our first date: one evening at a Pizza Express, when asked if he'd like anything to drink, he responded, 'Loads of red wine.' What a joyous order. How does a waiter interpret that? We did receive loads of red wine, so it worked. Barry is obsessed with pub etiquette. Barney Ronay once put a pint on the side of a pool table after a live show, and Barry went berserk.

Best thing about Barry?
In a world in which football broadcasting is full of sensationalist hyperbole, I really think his is an important voice. And his total honesty. Too many people bluff when they don't know. It is OK not to know.

Would you introduce him to your friends?
I have tried. I invited him to my wedding party. He texted the day before that it wasn't for him but maintains he is insulted not to have been invited. To be clear, my wedding was family only. He paints himself as the victim.

Describe Barry in three words.
Solid. Content. There.

What do you think he made of you?
A generic, conformist, leftie, vanilla snowflake.

Did you go on somewhere?
After our first meeting, no. But after a few cover shifts on the pod, when asked who I wanted to co-host my radio show, I knew he'd be the perfect foil: zero aspirations to sit in the hard chair but completely capable of delivering the best line/question after doing literally none of the heavy lifting.

And . . . did you kiss?
No. We have hugged twice, though: once when I moved to Australia; once on the first show we did after a challenging six weeks with an Olympic champion cyclist and knight of the realm.

If you could change one thing about the recording, what would it be?
Occasionally I would like it if he just answered the banal open goal of a question I ask him.

Marks out of 10?
9. There is something deeply alluring about him that I can't quite explain.

Would you meet again?
We meet on Zoom four times a week. I spend more time with Barry than I do with anyone else on Earth, apart from my wife and son Ian.

Being a referee isn't what it used to be. Not only have law changes and video technology changed the job beyond recognition, but in an age of tribalism and trial by social media the humble ref has become a hunted species. And so what better time to update an old classic? Presenting . . .

YOU ARE THE PGMOL-APPOINTED MATCH OFFICIAL

1. During a fierce derby game, a striker for the home side shoots at goal from long range. A defender scrambles to try and block the shot, but as he does so his prosthetic arm detaches from his body and flies towards the ball, striking it just inside the penalty area. As the home fans roar for a penalty, the defender argues that as his prosthetic arm went forwards rather than to the side, it was still part of his natural silhouette, and therefore a penalty should not be awarded. What is your decision?

4. Driving home in your excrement-and-urine-daubed car, you turn on the radio to hear an ex-referee – a former colleague of yours and someone you had long considered a friend – describe your performance as 'appalling' and claim that you should never be allowed to referee at the top level again. This man was a guest at your wedding. You've been on refereeing seminars together. You're the godfather to his two children. How should you feel?

2. The video assistant referee studies the incident for a couple of minutes and then orders you to watch it again on the replay screen. You jog to the touchline to consult the screen, but during the first replay the unit abruptly stops working and will not restart. Meanwhile, the home manager is claiming that a member of the away team's backroom staff deliberately vandalised the replay screen as soon as the VAR became involved. Play has now been stopped for several minutes, and the crowd is in open revolt. What action do you take?

3. After the game, you return to the car park to discover that your car has been smeared in excrement and urine by fans who are furious at some of your decisions. You spot the fans inquestion a few yards away, laughing and slapping each other on the back. One of them is filming you on his phone. It quickly becomes apparent that your reaction is being streamed live on Instagram. What is your next move?

5. The following morning, you are woken by the sound of shouting outside your window. Following your performance in the derby the previous evening, one disgruntled fan has posted your address on a forum, and already a small mob has formed, banging and kicking at your door. You pick up your phone to find 1,491 missed calls from withheld numbers. Yes, your phone number has also been published online. How do you react?

7. The public mood has turned ugly. Whipped up by a media frenzy over your handball decision, the angry mob has swollen in number. Pictures of you have been pinned to trees and lamp posts. Talk-show hosts are calling for your head. The local MP has vowed to track you down and bring you to justice. Your whimpering partner orders you to leave the house immediately, which you do under cover of darkness, via the back gate. Where do you go?

6. Later that day, your two teenage daughters come home early from school, both in floods of tears. They have been identified online and are being sent hundreds of death threats by angry fans. Citing the security of their fellow pupils, the school has ordered them not to attend until further notice. Sobbing and resentful, your girls beg you to quit your job. Ever since you were a child, refereeing has been your vocation and your dream. What do you do?

8. Shivering and homeless, you shuffle past a dilapidated industrial estate as dawn breaks. You hear sirens and helicopters in the distance, the feral roar of bloodthirsty vigilantes swarming the streets in their thousands, perhaps even tens of thousands. As you take shelter in the corrugated doorway of an aggregates manufacturing plant, you hear a whisper. A man in a suit, standing just a few yards away in the shadow of a parked Range Rover, offers you sanctuary if you step into his car. You are not sure whether to trust him. Do you get in the car?

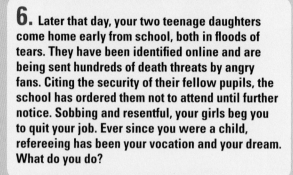

9. The Range Rover rolls through the lawless city streets. Through the blacked-out windows you can see throngs of furious football bans burning effigies of you and staging mock executions. The car pulls up outside a vast media complex. You are led wordlessly to an upstairs boardroom, where the producer of a nightly football panel discussion show offers you a regular, well-paid job analysing the refereeing incidents of the day. There is just one condition: you must be as scathing and unsympathetic towards your former colleagues as it is humanly possible to be. What is your decision?

JONATHAN LIEW

Football Weekly

FIFA: THE INSIDE STORY

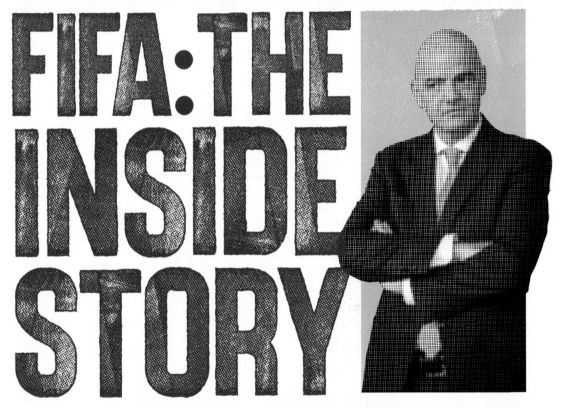

It was supposed to be a day like any other day for FIFA president Gianni Infantino.

The Qatar Airways private jet which had taken him from ▮▮▮▮ to ▮▮▮ to visit ▮ ▮▮▮▮▮▮▮▮▮▮▮ in Doha. To his surprise, ▮▮▮ rose from the runway still veiled by ▮▮▮▮▮▮▮▮ was there, waiting in the hotel the morning mist. Little did he know that ▮ lobby.

▮▮▮▮▮▮▮▮▮▮▮▮▮▮▮▮▮
▮▮▮▮▮▮▮▮▮▮▮▮▮▮▮▮▮
▮▮▮▮▮▮▮▮▮▮▮▮▮▮▮▮▮
▮▮▮▮▮▮▮▮▮▮▮ As to Vladimir ▮▮
▮▮▮▮▮▮▮▮▮▮▮▮▮▮▮▮▮

NEWS

██████████

██████████

'But who wouldn't accept ████████

██████████

████████ Surely nobody could think there was anything suspicious about that.' Although ████████

██████████

██████████ troop of Belarusian dancers ████████

██████████

████ Stoke City ██████████

██████████

████ to win the Champions League.

██████████

██████████ messages had been read. ████████ black BMW.

██████████

██████████ A bottle of Château Cheval Blanc 1990 appeared on the table, which had been ordered by ████████

██████████

██████████

At which point ████████

██████████

off,' he replied.

██████████

██████████

██████████ utter bastards.

construction magnate ████████

████ Patrice Motsepe ████████

██████████

██████████ truffle oil ████

████ Jack Warner ████████

██████████ integrity commission. ████

outrageous paper bag. ████████ revenue ████

██████████ World Cup ████████

██████████

██████████

Philippe Auclair, in ████

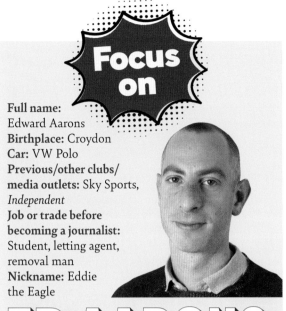

Full name: Edward Aarons
Birthplace: Croydon
Car: VW Polo
Previous/other clubs/media outlets: Sky Sports, *Independent*
Job or trade before becoming a journalist: Student, letting agent, removal man
Nickname: Eddie the Eagle

ED AARONS

Favourite player: Wilfried Zaha
A player for the future: Jesurun Rak-Sakyi
Favourite other podcast: *Made in Africa…!*
Childhood football hero: Ian Wright
Favourite other sports: Cricket, tennis, golf, rugby
Other sportsperson you most admire: Roger Federer
All-time favourite XI: Julián Speroni; Cafu, Joachim Andersen, Lucas Radebe, Dean Gordon; Paul Gascoigne, Claude Makélélé, Jay-Jay Okocha; Wilfried Zaha, Ronaldo (Brazilian), Sadio Mané
Most memorable match: Crystal Palace 4, Everton 1 (aet), 1991 Zenith Data Systems Cup final
Biggest disappointment: England 1, Germany 4, 2010 World Cup, Bloemfontein, South Africa
Best stadium visited: Maracanã
Favourite food and drink: Chicken Chettinad; dark rum (Havana Club 7 year old) and ginger ale
Miscellaneous likes: Sunshine, gardening
Miscellaneous dislikes: Rain and constant, unnecessary use of the word 'literally'
Favourite music: Drum and bass
Favourite actor: Sean Bean
Favourite actress: Helen Mirren
Favourite holiday destination: Jamaica
Best film seen recently: *A Game of Secrets* (Football Leaks documentary)
Favourite TV show: *Curb Your Enthusiasm*
Favourite activity on day off: Some kind of sport
Biggest influence on career: Steve Coppell
Superstitions: Used to have some lucky pants
International honours: None
Personal ambition: Survive the rising cost of living
If not a journalist, what would you do? Have to get up early
Which person in the world would you most like to meet? Viv Richards

Full name: Jordan Jarrett-Bryan
Birthplace: Brixton, London
Car: What car?
Previous/other clubs/media outlets: Channel 4 and Blakademik
Job or trade before becoming a journalist: Kitchen porter and stockroom sleeper at JD Sports
Nickname: JJB/Hot Takes King
Favourite player: Zinedine Zidane
A player for the future: Jacob Ramsey
Favourite other podcast: *Know Mercy* with Stephen A. Smith
Childhood football hero: Ian Wright
Favourite other sports: Tennis
Other sportsperson you most admire: Serena Williams
All-time favourite XI: Petr Čech; Branislav Ivanović, Lilian Thuram, Sol Campbell, Ashley Cole; Luís Figo, Yaya Touré, Gilberto Silva, Leroy Sané; Gabriel Batistuta, Dougie Freedman
Most memorable match: Brazil 1, Germany 7, World Cup semi-final, Belo Horizonte, 2014. Or Reading 5, Arsenal 7, League Cup fourth round, Reading, 2012
Biggest disappointment: Arsenal vs Barcelona, Champions League final, 2006
Best stadium visited: Selhurst Park
Favourite food and drink: Spag bol and elderflower
Miscellaneous dislikes: Pundits who chat shit (ironic, right)
Favourite music: Drum and bass
Favourite actor: Denzel Washington
Favourite holiday destination: Mombasa, Kenya
Best film seen recently: *Goodfellas*
Favourite TV show: *The Office* (UK)
Favourite activity on a day off: Sauna
Biggest influence on career: Max Rushden
Superstitions: Black shorts on a date
International honours: World Journalist of the Year
Personal ambition: Space Journalist of the Year
If not a journalist, what would you do? Psychologist
Which person in the world would you most like to meet? Nia Long

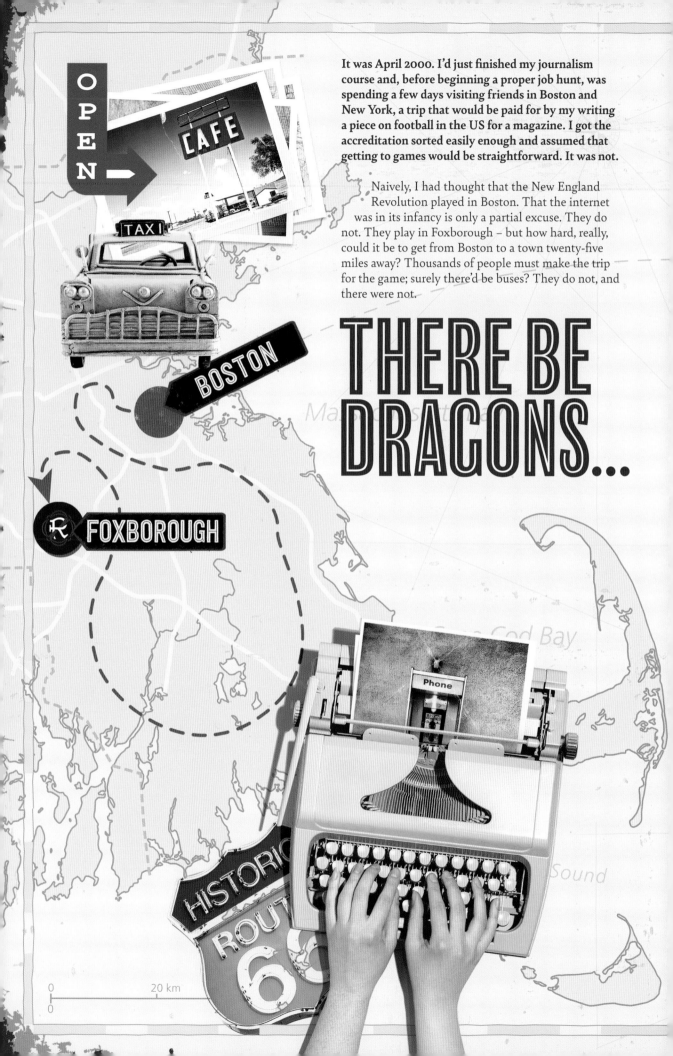

It was April 2000. I'd just finished my journalism course and, before beginning a proper job hunt, was spending a few days visiting friends in Boston and New York, a trip that would be paid for by my writing a piece on football in the US for a magazine. I got the accreditation sorted easily enough and assumed that getting to games would be straightforward. It was not.

Naively, I had thought that the New England Revolution played in Boston. That the internet was in its infancy is only a partial excuse. They do not. They play in Foxborough – but how hard, really, could it be to get from Boston to a town twenty-five miles away? Thousands of people must make the trip for the game; surely there'd be buses? They do not, and there were not.

THERE BE DRAGONS...

OPEN

CAFE

TAXI

BOSTON

Ⓡ FOXBOROUGH

Phone

HISTORIC ROUTE 6

0   20 km

I looked at a map. The nearest train station to Foxborough seemed to be Walpole, six miles to the north. There'd be shuttles from there, surely? So I took the train, mildly concerned that nobody else on board seemed to be heading for the football, and got off at Walpole. It was dark and lashing down with rain. Nobody else got off. In fact, there was nobody else about at all. I left the station. There was nothing there, just a station, a road and a forest. And it was really raining.

In the distance, I could make out a faint glow, so I set off through the trees towards it. It all felt very *Blair Witch*. I came to a small village green, where the Stars and Stripes flew at half mast, a Vietnam MIA flag above it. It was deserted. I came to the conclusion that there was no shuttle service. A man in a hunting jacket approached, a rifle slung over his shoulder. 'Excuse me,' I said, anxiously, hopelessly. 'Don't suppose there's a bus to the soccer game?'

'A what?'

'A bus to the soccer game?'

'Soccer game?' He looked thoughtful, as though he had heard the term before but couldn't quite remember where.

'In Foxborough?'

'A bus to the soccer game?' He laughed uproariously, as though this were the most ridiculous concept in the world. I told him I was a journalist, and he gave me the card of a taxi service and pointed to a phone booth. 'That's your only chance,' he said, and walked off through the rain.

The taxi company seemed mystified by the idea of taking me from Walpole to Foxborough but agreed to do so. It would, though, take them half an hour to get to Walpole, so I wandered off, looking for somewhere to get out of the rain and perhaps get something to eat. I found a brightly lit takeaway pizza place with a couple of tables in the front and was wiping my feet and shaking the worst of the rain from my hair when I saw the man in the hunting jacket sitting at the counter. Between guffaws, he told the young woman at the till that I was a journalist going to the soccer game, then urged her to get the boss.

The boss was an alarming-looking man, tall and cadaverous, dressed entirely in black, with slicked-back hair that was just beginning to grey at the temples – a pizza-shop owner played by Christopher Lee. 'Show him!' the man in the hunting jacket urged, and, eventually, the manager agreed. I was, it's fair to say, thoroughly unnerved, so to avoid eye contact with anybody, I began inspecting the walls. There were two signed photographs, one of Kevin Bacon and one

of Marvin Hagler. Both dedications referred to 'the Dragons' – some Little League Baseball team, perhaps? The boss returned, carrying a blue plastic box, out of which he took a small remote-controlled quad bike. Then he reached into his shirt. At that moment, thoroughly spooked, I had no idea what he might pull out. A knife? A gun? Was life to end in a pool of blood in a brightly lit pizza shop in the middle of nowhere, Massachusetts? But he took out what, to my untutored eye, appeared to be an iguana, though I later learned it was a bearded dragon. He dropped it onto the bike. It clearly knew what it was doing, clutching the handlebars and clenching its knees against the chassis, a frown of concentration on its face. The boss put it on the floor and began to drive it about.

'I was on *Letterman* with this,' he said. 'Course, on *Letterman* we had a pig on the controls.'

The taxi arrived, and I finally took my seat in the press box just as the game was kicking off. A short, athletic man in the seat next to me shook my hand enthusiastically. '*I'm* Ferdie,' he said, in a way that made it clear I should know who Ferdie was.

I apologised for my ignorance, explaining I'd come from London. It turned out he was something of a local celebrity, having played professional football on five continents, and held world records for both speed keepie-ups and running the 100m backwards.

Which is all very well and, in normal circumstances, might have been very impressive. But that day, if you hadn't trained a pig to drive a bearded dragon about on a remote-controlled quad bike, I just wasn't interested.

JONATHAN WILSON

JOÃO HAVELANGE'S MORAL MAZE

You are born, aged 0, naturally programmed with a self-serving and monomaniacal world view. A promising start.

Take afternoon nap.
← MISS THREE TURNS

GET OUT OF BOTHER CARD

Coffee, petits fours.

Accept honorary title from president of emerging petro-nation.

GET OUT OF BOTHER CARD

MEDIA FLASHPOINT!
You suggest women should play in high heels and skimpy things.
► PLAY GOOD CARD OR MISS TURN ►

GET OUT OF BOTHER CARD

GET OUT OF BOTHER CARD

Accept honorary medal from president of established superpower.
► FORWARD TWO PLACES

Your sports marketing firm collapses with debts of 130 million Swiss francs. Heads of 130 million Swiss francs.
► QUIETLY TRANSFERRED OFFSHORE
► MISS ONE TURN WHILE MONIES ARE QUIETLY TRANSFERRED OFFSHORE

'WOTCHER, KIDS!
Jean-Marie Faustin Godefroid de Havelange here . . . but you can call me João! You may remember me for my twenty-four-year reign as president of FIFA, my forty-eight-year stint as a member of the IOC, and my extensive code-of-ethics-compliant collection of diamonds, paintings and *objets d'art*. But if you're thinking, "Cripes, cor, life as a sports administrator looks a right doss!" let me warn you: while I may have turned desecrating the world's greatest football tournaments with fizzy-drink branding, funnelling monies into opaque offshore enterprises and glad-handing tinpot politicians into an art form, it ain't as easy as it looks.
SO, COULD YOU GET TO THE TOP LIKE ME?
ROLL THE DICE, AND WE SHALL SEE!'

PANG OF CONSCIENCE!
► GO BACK TO START ►

OUT OF
R CARDS

MEDIA FLASHPOINT!
Emergence of thirty-year-old photo of you in blackface and dressed as a Nazi.
► PLAY GOOD CARD OR MISS TURN ►

Your vote swings the 2034 World Cup for the Isle of Man.
► BACK EIGHT SPACES ►

SACK OF OATMEAL CARD:
all those mealy-mouthed responses you have to give.

BRASS NECK CARD:
Get the self-confidence to say or do anything you please and be blissfully unaware of the offence caused.

EARPLUG CARD:
Protection against all the naysayers, detractors and general negativity that you may attract.

SHOULDER PADS CARD:
Power-up your shrug to new levels of total disregard.

HOTSHOT LAWYER CARD:
Access to the best legal advice when you find yourself in a bind.

Beef Wellington, hand-dived scallops with white truffles, champagne.

MEDIA FLASHPOINT!
Expenses claim for Zurich escort agency leaked.
► PLAY GOOD CARD OR MISS TURN ►

You fill your nappy with shit. Congratulations, you have landed a seat on the FIFA congress!

GET OUT OF BOTHER CARD

GET OUT OF BOTHER CARD

You put forward an unworkable plan for a 128-team World Cup.
◄ BACK ONE SPACE

MEDIA FLASHPOINT! Your opening ceremony speech is complete bollocks.
◄ PLAY GooB CARD OR MISS TURN ►

Brown envelope containing Mitteleuropean currency!
◄ FORWARD TWO SPACES

TV RIGHTS. You award them to your own sports marketing firm.
FORWARD SIX SPACES ►

MEDIA FLASHPOINT! Your mobility scooter mows down four children as you fight your way to the buffet.
◄ PLAY GooB CARD OR MISS TURN ►

PANG OF CONSCIENCE! but you have long forgotten what those feel like.
FORWARD ONE SPACE ►

PANG OF CONSCIENCE!
GO BACK TO START ►

PANG OF CONSCIENCE!
GO BACK TO START ►

CONGRATS!
YOU ARE THE PRESIDENT OF ALL FOOTBALL!
You will sleep like a baby every night and die a free man, aged 103.

GET OUT OF BOTHER CARD

GET OUT OF BOTHER CARD

Agents! You press on for your career funds.

You feel like a migrant worker.
You are dead.
GAME OVER ►

TV RIGHTS. You accidentally put them out to open tender.
BACK ONE SPACE ►

Goodie bag on hotel bed.
FORWARD TWO PLACES ►

GET OUT OF BOTHER CARD

MB
MAX BARRY

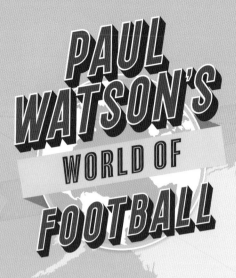

PAUL WATSON'S WORLD OF FOOTBALL

PAUL WATSON was a semi-professional footballer who in 2007 decided he would try to become an international by applying to the lowest-ranked team on the planet, the Federated States of Micronesia. Realising that Micronesian naturalisation laws made that impossible, he instead turned to coaching, becoming manager of the island of Pohnpei. Since then, his career has taken him on a journey through some of football's more obscure corners.

MATCH-FIXING IN MOLDOVA

Over the last few years, approaches from clubs in exotic locations have become the norm. Through various TV production companies, I was offered chances to manage a North Korean side and coach an uncontacted tribe in Papua New Guinea. I didn't turn either job down as such but, unsurprisingly, neither materialised.

One job offer that came much closer to fruition arrived from Moldova. A club that had recently been relegated from the top flight approached me to become their sporting director, charged with reviving their fortunes. The conversations over a slightly erratic phone line went well, until I was introduced to their chairman, who seemed a lot less friendly. He wanted to know if I was able to recruit players from Africa and Asia, and was keen to stress that my modest salary was irrelevant because it could be supplemented by a series of 'performance bonuses', which I took to mean 'in the event of promotion'.

Communication sputtered out over the next few months, and I eventually forgot all about my Moldovan flirtation, until around a year later, when I read that the club had disbanded following a raft of match-fixing allegations. I may have had a lucky escape.

TAXI TROUBLE

On the way to a coaching job in Mongolia, I had a day's layover in Bishkek, the capital of Kyrgyzstan. I arrived in the early hours of the morning and hailed a taxi outside the airport, with no idea of the language, the currency or where my hotel was. The driver, after discovering I was English, started firing off the names of football clubs at me – 'West Ham . . . Liverpool . . .' – and I nodded my head in tired agreement. After a while, he started to repeatedly emit a long, threatening gurgle, while gesturing increasingly wildly and, to my horror, removing his hands from the wheel for long periods.

To make matters worse, it became clear that we were headed away from Bishkek. With no way to communicate, I started to think something was amiss, especially when we pulled up at a residential address in a deserted, dark street. The driver gestured for me to follow him. Sure I was being kidnapped, I agreed, while pondering my method of escape.

We went into a house, and the driver flicked on a light, ushering me into a room. Inside was a veritable shrine to Manchester United, with ageing posters of the team on the walls, alongside a framed shirt and a pennant. The driver tapped on a picture, apparently his prized possession, and again emitted his guttural grunt. I squinted at a signed photo of Wayne Rooney, and finally it dawned on me that the sound he'd been making for the last half-hour was in fact 'Rooney'. Satisfied, he led me back to the car and drove me to my hotel in silence.

THE SIMON COWELL OF MONGOLIA

After returning from Pohnpei, I was not exactly inundated with offers of jobs in the world of football management, so when an email arrived from a Mongolian businessman called Enkhjin ('Enki') Batsumber in 2013, asking me to help set up a flagship team for a new breakaway Mongolian football league, I decided I had to do it. Shortly afterwards, I was on a plane heading for Ulaanbaatar, which I was to belatedly discover is the world's coldest capital city. On arrival, it turned out there was a slight hitch. The sponsors for the team had dropped out, so we had no players, no stadium to play in, not even a football to our name. Fortunately, Enki was a resourceful man. He marched into the offices of one of Mongolia's biggest TV channels without an appointment and pitched a TV show in which we would build a team via *American Idol*-style try-outs.

Incredibly, it worked. We were commissioned to produce *Dream Team*, which was sponsored by an almost undrinkable soft drink. I would judge the hopefuls and was told to be 'the Simon Cowell of Mongolia'. Although the producers spoke almost no English and I had no Mongolian, they insisted it wouldn't be a problem, as one of Mongolia's hit TV shows of the 1980s was a Venezuelan soap opera that nobody could understand.

Sadly, the sponsor pulled out after six episodes, denying the world more televisual gold.

HEADLIGHTS FOR FLOODLIGHTS

In 2019, on the Micronesian island of Pohnpei, we set up a football league, which we grandly named the Pohnpei Premier League. We went around the island looking for community groups who might enter a team. We even (unsuccessfully) cold-called a Mormon hut at one stage in a bid to find enough teams.

Despite some teething problems, such as teams turning up according to 'island time' (an hour after kick-off) and the pitch being overrun by toads, the league was a big success. However, at half-time in the final game of the season, the two remaining ancient floodlights gave in and plunged us into darkness.

With the season's showpiece fixture on the line, we came up with a very grassroots solution that would enable our Premier League to reach its conclusion: the players all drove their cars to the touchline and put on their headlights. The game was completed, the Island Pitbulls triumphed, and several car batteries went flat.

Full name: Mark Langdon
Birthplace: East, east, east London
Car: Ford Fiesta
Previous/other clubs/media outlets: The first rule of previous clubs is don't talk about previous clubs
Job or trade before becoming a journalist: Handing out leaflets for a dodgy shop that sold counterfeit designer clothes
Nickname: Lango
Favourite newspaper: *Racing Post*
Favourite player: Roberto Baggio

Focus on

MARK LANGDON

A player for the future: Roméo Lavia at Southampton
Childhood football hero: Gazza
Other sportsperson you most admire: Snooker player Mark Williams
All-time favourite XI: Gigi Buffon; Dani Alves, Ledley King, Alessandro Nesta, Paolo Maldini; Gazza, Mousa Dembélé; Lionel Messi, Roberto Baggio, Kylian Mbappé; Brazilian Ronaldo
Most memorable match: Ajax 2, Tottenham 3, Champions League semi-final, second leg, Amsterdam, 2019
Biggest disappointment: Life is one long disappointment
Friendliest away fans: Hate them all
Best stadium played in: Craven Cottage
Favourite food and drink: Meat and beer
Miscellaneous dislikes: Vegetables
Favourite singer: Usher
Favourite actor: Neymar
Favourite holiday destination: Orlando
Best film seen recently: *A Star Is Born*
Favourite TV show: *Only Murders in the Building* and *The White Lotus*
Favourite activity on a day off: Er . . .
Biggest influence on career: Richard Keys
International honours: I've been on Stan Sport in Australia and beIN
Personal ambition: To be famous enough to appear on the *Off Menu* podcast
If not a journalist, what would you do? Postman
Which person in the world would you most like to meet? Gary Neville, and I'd keep asking him questions until I found a subject on which he didn't think he was an expert

---

Full name: Faye Carruthers
Birthplace: Luton
Car: Kia Sportage
Previous/other clubs/media outlets: talkSPORT, Sky Sports, BBC Sport, Absolute Radio

Focus on

FAYE CARRUTHERS

Job or trade before becoming a journalist: PA, lifeguard, chilli picker
Nickname: Fayezee, Carruthers, Holy Carruthers
Favourite player: Mick Harford
A player for the future: Jobe Bellingham
Favourite other podcast: *Guardian Women's Football Weekly*
Childhood football hero: Andrei Kanchelskis
Favourite other sports: Netball, tennis, rugby
Other sportsperson you most admire: Dame Kelly Holmes
All-time favourite XI: In no particular order and in absolutely no formation: Carlos Valderrama, Stuart Pearce, Steve McNulty, Ian Wright, Claude Gnakpa, Kingsley Black, Andrei Kanchelskis, Paul Gascoigne, Mick Harford, Steve Howard, Roger Milla
Most memorable match: Can I have two?! Luton 3, Scunthorpe 2 (aet), Johnstone's Paint Trophy final, 2009; England 2, Germany 1 (aet), Women's Euro 2022 final
Biggest disappointment: Luton's relegation from the Football League; England losing the Euro 2020 final
Best stadium visited: San Siro
Favourite food and drink: Paella, G&T
Miscellaneous likes: Kind, thoughtful people
Miscellaneous dislikes: Grapefruit
Favourite music: Prodigy
Favourite actor: David Tennant
Favourite actress: Kristen Wiig
Favourite holiday destination: Maldives
Best film seen recently: *Elvis*
Favourite TV show: *The Handmaid's Tale*
Favourite activity on day off: Gym and spa
Biggest influence on career: My mum
Superstitions: So many – I'm weird!
International honours: I won AU$100 for writing an article for *The Word* backpackers magazine about the 2003 Rugby World Cup (I know – still dining off it!)
Personal ambition: To walk the Inca Trail
If not a journalist, what would you do? Interior designer
Which person in the world would you most like to meet? Eric Morecambe

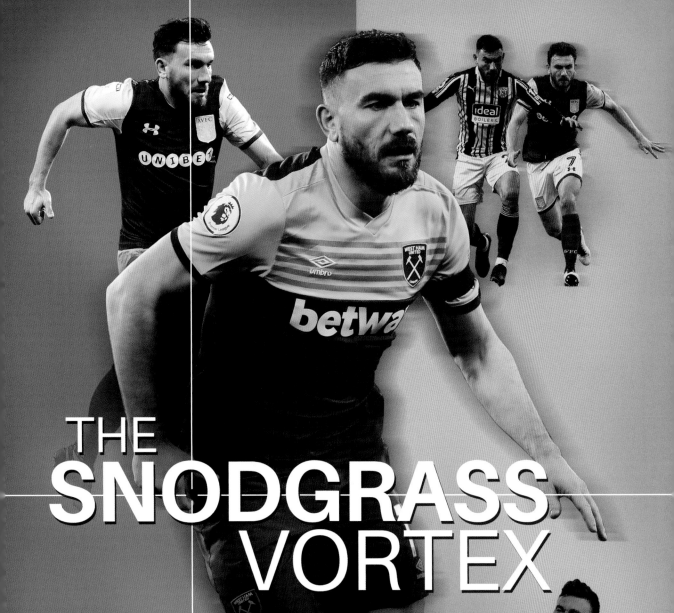

ROBERT SNODGRASS IS ROBERT SNODGRASS

THE
SNODGRASS
VORTEX

GUARDIAN PICTURES PRESENTS A RUSHDEN/GLENDENNING PRODUCTION. A JONATHAN WILSON FILM ROBERT SNODGRASS
'THE SNODGRASS VORTEX' ROBERT SNODGRASS ROBERT SNODGRASS ROBERT SNODGRASS ROBERT SNODGRASS
ROBERT SNODGRASS MUSIC BY LIAM McCLAIR MUSIC SUPERVISOR PHILIPPE AUCLAIR VISUAL EFFECTS SUPERVISOR ROBERT SNODGRASS
EDITOR ROBERT SNODGRASS PRODUCTION DESIGN ROBERT SNODGRASS DIRECTOR OF PHOTOGRAPHY ROBERT SNODGRASS
PRODUCED BY JOEL SILAS AND LUCY BASED ON THE NOVEL BY ROBERT SNODGRASS EXECUTIVE PRODUCERS CHRISTIAN BENNETT
DANIELLE STEPHENS MAX SANDERSON SCREENPLAY MAX RUSHDEN AND BARRY GLENDENNING

www.snodgrassvortex.com DIRECTED BY ROBERT SNODGRASS

TO BE PERFECTLY HONEST... WITH TROY TOWNSEND

Each of the following questions features four possible answers, only one of which is true. Can you separate the fiction from the totally honest?

1 The first name of the England World Cup winner Ray Wilson was . . .

a) Randolph
b) Ramon
c) Ralph
d) Ernest

2 In 2003, Nicolae Cringus, the chairman of Romanian fourth-division club Steaua Nicolae Bălcescu, proposed tackling repeated pitch invasions by installing . . .

a) an electric fence
b) a moat filled with crocodiles
c) snipers armed with stun guns
d) a wall of fire

3 In 1998, in a game between Bristol City and Wolves, there was a half-time brawl between . . .

a) Wolves' wolf mascot and three little pigs, representing a local double-glazing firm
b) a St John Ambulance crew and a local choir
c) two Wolves substitutes and six home ballboys
d) four fans called from the crowd for a penalty shoot-out

4 Guillermo Stábile, top scorer in the 1930 World Cup, only came into the Argentina side because the first choice, Nolo Ferreira, returned home . . .

a) to complete his law exams
b) to look after his ailing grandmother
c) to escape a Montevideo loan shark
d) to play in a lucrative polo match

5 The early Sunderland director Samuel Tyzack would scout Scottish clubs for talent incognito by disguising himself as . . .

a) a priest
b) a circus performer
c) a doctor
d) a travelling brush salesman

6 Alain Gouaméné, the goalkeeper who kept clean sheets in every match as Ivory Coast won the 1992 Africa Cup of Nations, would . . .

a) keep an elephant's tooth in his boot
b) sing the Ivorian anthem backwards
c) kiss the defender Sam Abouo on the head as they left the dressing room
d) urinate on the goalposts at the beginning of each half

7 Herbert Bamlett became Manchester United manager in 1927. What role had he earlier played in the club's history?

a) He had suggested replacing their green-and-yellow shirts with red
b) He had reported the illegal payments by Manchester City that allowed United to sign four of their best players
c) He had saved the life of the goalkeeper Alf Steward during the First World War
d) He had been the referee who had abandoned an FA Cup tie in which United were trailing to Burnley in 1908–9, the season they won the competition for the first time

8 During his time at Norwich City the striker Dion Dublin briefly shared a flat with . . .

a) Jason Statham
b) Mick Channon
c) Ed Balls
d) Bernard Matthews

9 Alvin Martin's hat-trick against Newcastle United in 1986 was . . .

a) comprised entirely of headers
b) scored against three different goalkeepers
c) the only time he ever scored for West Ham
d) scored despite him struggling to see because a contact lens had fallen out

10 A play-off for the 1933 Uruguayan league title between Peñarol and Nacional was abandoned following a brawl prompted by . . .

a) a dog belonging to the Nacional manager biting the Peñarol goalkeeper
b) Peñarol's goalkeeper pulling down the crossbar as a Nacional shot flew just over
c) a Nacional player riling the Peñarol captain, claiming that his wife was having an affair
d) a goal being given to Peñarol, even though the ball had gone out of play and then rebounded off a case belonging to Nacional's team doctor

11 The boots David Beckham was wearing when he scored his goal from the halfway line against Wimbledon were . . .

a) two sizes too big for him
b) embroidered with the name 'Charlie' because they had originally been made for the Rangers midfielder Charlie Miller
c) missing the Adidas insignia because of a contract dispute
d) painted black because Alex Ferguson felt the red and white trim was too eye-catching

13 Before becoming a coach, Francisco Maturana, who led Atlético Nacional to the Copa Libertadores and managed Colombia at the 1990 and 1994 World Cups, worked as a . . .

a) postman
b) astrophysicist
c) dentist
d) traffic warden

14 Which of the following never scored twenty Premier League goals in a single season?

a) Peter Beardsley
b) Didier Drogba
c) Louis Saha
d) Michael Owen

15 Gianfranco Zola's red card against Nigeria at the 1994 World Cup was notable because . . .

a) it was his international debut
b) it was the only card of his career
c) it was his birthday
d) he was the first Italian ever to be sent off in the tournament

16 At the 1966 World Cup, anthems were played only before the opening match and the final because . . .

a) there was a musicians' strike
b) the organisers wanted to ensure games kicked off promptly for television
c) the authorities didn't want to play the anthem of North Korea, which had not been formally recognised as a nation by the UK
d) anthems were deemed overly militaristic

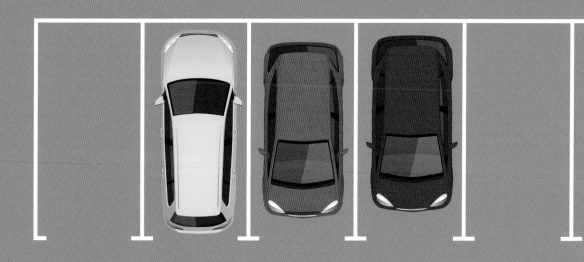

P BEN FISHER'S CAR PARKS OF BRITISH FOOTBALL ⬅

Since bursting onto the scene with his famously gripping story about the parking facilities at Newport County, Ben Fisher is now recognised as the UK's leading expert on football-club car parks. Here, he chooses five of his favourites

1. VITALITY STADIUM / DEAN COURT, AFC BOURNEMOUTH, BH7 7AF

Even the billionaire riches of American businessman Bill Foley have not changed the modest car park to the rear of the corrugated iron – and temporary – South Stand, erected in 2013. Until then, the ground was three-sided, à la Oxford United's Kassam Stadium. Premier League premiums do not apply here: fans pay just £1 for the privilege of parking directly behind the stand named after the former Bournemouth and Manchester United striker Ted MacDougall. Away supporters' coaches pull into the car park, also used by television outside-broadcast trucks, to drop off fans a couple of hours before kick-off. A typically warm Dorset welcome is guaranteed.

2. MADEJSKI STADIUM SELECT CAR LEASING STADIUM, READING FC, RG2 0FL

Fans stump up £230 for a season ticket in the Red Car Park, barely a couple of minutes' walk from the ground. A soulless stadium, but a brilliant, no-nonsense arrangement. In truth, it is a treat for the car-park aficionado. At the end of Biscuit Way (I know) is an endless haven of concrete bays in which to apply the handbrake. Supporters could be forgiven for not being quite so hot on the set-up, given the queues in the immediate aftermath of a game, but for anyone hanging around afterwards, a brisk departure is par for the course.

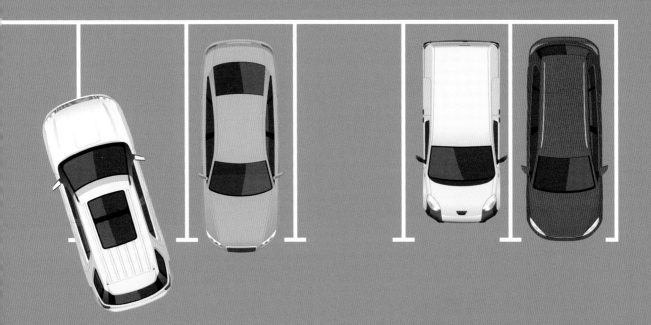

3. ADAMS PARK STADIUM, WYCOMBE WANDERERS, HP12 4HJ

At the end of the Sands Industrial Estate, this grey matter is nestled on the edge of the Chiltern Hills. The two-tier car park (the lower tier is boxed off for players, officials, hospitality and disabled guests) developed a notorious reputation after Wycombe were ridiculed online for confirming it had sold out against Sunderland last year. 'The maximum capacity is 350 in good weather, reduced to 150 in poor conditions,' says the club website.

4. LIBERTY STADIUM, SWANSEA CITY, SA1 2JT

If one cannot nab a spot in the stadium grounds themselves, then getting a space opposite the Landore Park and Ride, a few minutes' walk down the road, is the next best thing. Better still, Phil, a cheery steward, guarantees a warm Welsh reception on arrival at the media entrance. Not quite the 'muck and nettles' of the Championship that Neil Warnock speaks about in glowing terms, but rather a mix of gravel, the odd puddle and grass.

5. HUISH PARK, YEOVIL TOWN, BA22 8YF

There is something soothing about a trip to Somerset, even though Yeovil do possess, let's face it, a piddly stadium. While the club is now non-league, in the past big matches – Manchester United visited in the FA Cup in 2015 and 2018 – have meant parking on the grass verge behind the basic, uncovered terrace that houses the away fans. The Garden of Remembrance at the other end, where there are tributes to former striker Adam Stansfield, who died of cancer aged thirty-one, and former captain Lee Collins, who took his own life in 2021, is a nice touch.

A Transcript of the Original Classic Anecdote

The Gate That Wasn't Locked in the Night-Time, Newport vs Brighton, 10 January 2021
'I'd parked in the primary school where the Newport players and staff park. That's where you can park on a match day at the moment. As I left the ground at about half past eleven last night, I was very worried that they might have locked it up, so I hotfooted it around the perimeter of Rodney Parade and sprinted to get there, with all the grace of Dan Burn, and eventually got there, and it was open. So I was very happy. I could get home safely, and here I am now. I lived to tell the tale. I worked up a sweat. I was thinking, "How can I get home?" All these things were rushing through my head.'

SLIPS & SNIPS

Over the years, when we've asked what people do while listening to *Football Weekly*, there has been a remarkable amount of correspondence on two subjects in particular: car crashes and vasectomies. While you draw your conclusions about just what that says about our listenership, here are some of the best emails on those themes . . .

CAR CRASHES...

ALEX 1

In January this year, on my way home from a late shift at work and with the pod on the car Bluetooth, I hit a pothole and then black ice. The car went into a skid and then into a wall on a country road. I was completely unhurt, but the gearbox, steering column, fuel tank, suspension and engine were all ruined and the car written off. Despite all this damage, while sitting in the smoking ruin of my car in disbelief that I was unharmed, the pod continued to play on the undamaged stereo system like nothing had happened.

DAVID

I too have had a car crash while listening to the pod. I remember getting out of the car, and all I could hear were Max and Sid laughing in the background.

JAMES

On a narrow country lane, a van came around the corner too fast for me to see. I swerved up the steep grass verge in an unsuccessful attempt to avoid the van, and this meant I was trapped in the car, balanced precariously. Too scared to move for fear of tipping over, I had to sit completely still until the van driver came to my aid, listening for what felt like an age to Gregg Bakowski recount how he felt as Liverpool conceded their third in the Champions League final of 2005. In that moment, I really did not have an ounce of sympathy for Gregg.

ALEX 2

I had a car crash while listening. My little Aygo was written off, but *Football Weekly* kept playing through the aux cable.

PATRICK

While attempting to reverse down my drive, and listening to the pod, I put the car into the wrong gear and accelerated up a bank, flipping the car onto its roof. All three emergency services had to be called and the car was a write-off, but I emerged unscathed. Annoyingly, the podcast kept playing throughout, so I had to listen to it all over again, from the beginning.

DAN

I'd like to stake a claim for the most pathetic car crash while listening to the pod. We have heard about people crawling from wreckage or balancing precariously on grassy mounds, but my story is the equivalent of Ben Fisher's car-park anecdote. I once crashed into half a lamp post at around 2 mph after leaving my local barbershop. I had got into the car, and the opening music of the pod hadn't even finished before the crash had taken place. I can't blame any one of you, but rather my terrible driving, lack of awareness and the distraction of my new haircut.

JAY

In early December 2019, I was driving home from guitar tutoring along some poorly lit lanes on a horrible dark rainy evening, listening to *Football Weekly* via my phone speaker. As I was waiting to pull out, a fellow road user misjudged the turning and slammed into the side of my car. I had the full car-crash experience with air bags and smoke but thankfully wasn't injured, so I hopped out and made sure he was OK. As I went back into my car to get my phone, the podcast was still playing, so instead of standing in the rain I just rolled the seat back, pushed the airbags out of the way and finished the episode while waiting for the recovery truck.

JOE

Around two years ago, I was in the midst of my final year at the University of Sussex, very low on sleep and cycling to campus. In Brighton, there is a cycle lane that is usually pretty safe, going from the town all the way up to the campus next to the Amex Stadium. However, portions of it are shared with a bus lane. It was a particularly windy day, and I had my earphones in, listening to the pod. To shield my face I was looking down at my pedals, when I crashed head-first into the back of a parked bus. I gathered myself while hearing Max and Barry chuckling about something in my ears, got back on my bike and decided to cycle past the bus, only to see the driver along with all the passengers chuckling along in unison with Max and Barry. Felt like a right mug.

ANDREW 1

I'm currently listening to Elis James gush over Wales's recent success while recovering from a vasectomy. When I told one of my brothers I was going in for the operation, he said, 'Oh, your testicles are getting relegated.' He extended the metaphor to our other brother, who, in recently converting to Catholicism, has joined a super league without any promotion or relegation. The philosopher Nicolas Bourriaud says that artists make art to understand the world around them. Have you found yourself using football to understand the world? Will I forever have to refer to these parts of my body as Norwich City or Newcastle, depending on how the table turns out?

MATTHEW

I had a vasectomy today. Since I wouldn't be asleep under general anaesthesia, I asked if I could use an earbud to listen to some music. I didn't really want to hear anything. So while the urologist performed the procedure, I listened to Max and the panel discuss how awful Everton are. So thanks for the distraction as it was much better hearing the pod than any noises while they cut and cauterised my bits. It made a vas deferens to the experience.

ANDREW 2

After having our second child about a year ago, my wife and I decided it was time for the snip. I intentionally scheduled my appointment on a Friday so I would have the weekend to rest up and watch some sports, before returning to the office on Monday. Or so I thought . . .

Liverpool were playing Huddersfield, and as I reclined to start the procedure I pulled the match up on my phone and started to watch. A couple of quick Liverpool goals made it somewhat uninteresting and not as distracting as I had hoped, so I decided to switch to the pod from earlier in the week. That's more or less when it started . . .

They do one testicle at a time. First one went smoothly – 10 mins tops, and we were on to ball number two. After about 15 mins I was starting to get somewhat curious about what was going on. Doc mentioned he had to run out and would be back in a minute or two.

Me: You gotta take a piss or something?

Doc: Ha, no. Just one minute. [*returning with a colleague*] This is my colleague Dr . . . UH-OH.

I see concerned looks cross their faces. I've got one earbud in at this time, listening to you all talk about City's 20th straight win. They ask me to stop listening, they've got something important to say.

Doc: Can we use your phone to call your wife? I'd like to speak with her.

Me: Ah . . . what?

Doc: I'm sorry, but I've nicked a vein. It will probably heal on its own, but if it doesn't, you'll lose the testicle. So we're scheduling you for immediate surgery, and we need to make arrangements with your wife.

I'll spare you the rest . . . but the result was full-blown 'slice it open to fix it' surgery, not the much less invasive version of your typical vasectomy. I was off my feet for a week and wasn't able to return to normal activity for about 15 days. It was miserable, of course, but not nearly as frustrating as what happened next, as the US healthcare industry tried to charge me $30,000.

ADAM

Morning, gang, rather odd niche you are developing here, but on Boxing Day 2017 I listened to the Christmas special while being circumcised. You were a very calming distraction during the procedure, which has scarred me in many ways. Fast-forward four years, two kids and a pandemic later, I then listened during Easter 2022 while having a vasectomy. Hopefully I don't need another medical procedure around my gentlemen's agreement, but if I do I will be sure to 'get you involved'. Keep up the good work.

MARK

Having followed the updates by listeners on the uncomfortable situations they've found themselves in while listening to the show, knowing my vasectomy was coming I was quite excited to finally have a reason to send you a message. I was then devastated when the nurse told me that I couldn't bring a phone with me into the operating room. Now I'll never know if having my vas deferens cut while listening to you be unimpressed by West Ham's latest lacklustre performance would make me hate them more than I already do.

SILENT WITNESS

Silent Witness is the longest-running detective show in the world, amassing 228 episodes since it was first screened in 1996 and drawing obsessive fans, including Barry and Wilson. Its relationship with football in that time has been fitful, the increasing references to the game suggesting football's growing importance as a background cultural signifier over that period. Here we consider *Silent Witness*'s six most striking footballing moments.

The Mystery of the Recurring Neil Shipperley
(Season 2, episodes 1 and 4)

One evening, a man goes to visit a grieving neighbour. The television is on, and we see Neil Shipperley having a goal ruled out for Southampton in their 2–0 FA Cup quarter-final defeat at Manchester United on Monday, 11 March 1996. That seems plausible enough. But the game was broadcast by Sky, whose commentators were Martin Tyler and Andy Gray – yet the voice we hear is that of David Pleat. The former Tottenham manager's words weren't broadcast until the highlights on *Match of the Day*, screened on BBC One at 10.10 p.m. that night. The light, though, suggests this is a spring evening, and the implication is that the match is being watched live.

That would be puzzling enough, but in the following week's story, as a suspect sits in front of a television and his younger brothers play with toy guns, we just about hear Pleat's incredulity at the referee's decision once again. In itself, that's not problematic. Why wouldn't two people in Cambridge both be watching the same match? Except the pathologist Sam Ryan's relationship with Superintendent Ross, going well at the time of Pleat I, has all but collapsed by the time of Pleat II. What on earth is going on? Is Dr Ryan really so volatile?

The Chase at the Népstadion
(Season 14, episode 7)

Dr Harry Cunningham returns to the flat he is sharing in Budapest with the human rights lawyer Anna Sándor to find she has been stabbed to death. The killer hasn't left, and after a brief altercation, Harry is left covered in blood and clutching the knife. As suspicion falls on him, he flees the scene, then calls Duncan McBurney, his contact at the British embassy. He is on the corner of Eleonóra utca and Szobránc utca, so McBurney tells him to wait for him at the nearby stadium.

As he sits on the steps outside an office by the Népstadion, Harry is approached by a street hustler in a grubby red–brown suit and floral shirt. As he is shooing him away, a police car pulls up. Harry walks over, but the police drive off, slowing to a halt beside a dark blue car. As the officers talk to the driver, a shaven-headed man in sunglasses, Harry realises something is wrong, particularly as the hustler starts to make a run for it. Harry follows him, as the blue car sets off in pursuit. They head up the steps into the stadium, with two thugs giving chase. They turn left down some steps towards Entrance 4, at which point the car pulls up, forcing them back inside, towards the pitch. Harry gets away, and the hustler explains that the police and the mafia are in cahoots.

32

There seems no deeper significance to the presence of the stadium than that, even in its dilapidated state, with the banks of red, white and green seats in varying states of disrepair, the Népstadion is a scenic place to run around (it has since been replaced by the Ferenc Puskás Aréna, as part of Viktor Orbán's enormous investment into sport). We can, though, probably deduce that given Harry has apparently not crossed a major road, Sándor's flat is in Terézváros, perhaps just east of Andrássy út. Although that does mean Harry would have run through the relatively slim corridor between the city park and Keleti train station, the architecture seems to fit.

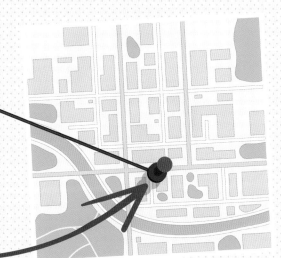

The One About the Footballer
(Season 17, episodes 1 and 2)

Isaac Dreyfus, a Jewish footballer who plays for Thames City, is arrested after the body of his missing au pair is discovered, having lain for several days under grass clippings in a skip at City's Duchess Meadows training ground.

Football is established as a theme early in the episode, when we see a Thames City scarf and a poster of Dreyfus on a boy's bedroom wall. The forensic scientist Jack Hodgson – who in Season 26 will refer to himself as a Linfield fan, logically enough given his upbringing in Belfast – then goes, alone, to a Thames City match, where he witnesses Dreyfus score, before being sent off for headbutting an opponent who had racially abused him. Football scenes in drama are never convincing, but while there is the familiar fault of a key figure being allowed to run much too far with the ball, and the referee has way too large a belly for a Premier League official, this isn't too bad. The crowd scenes, similarly, feel inauthentic, although it's hard to isolate precisely why. It's probably that their singing is too tuneful and their reactions too unanimous; it's all too clean.

Although the Emirates is used for the scenes involving club directors, the game itself is clearly played at the Valley, which tallies with Jack's comment that he is nearby when the au pair's body is found by the river. Later scenes in the empty stadium are careful to show only the 'FC' written in the seats, so we can imagine 'TC' existing where 'CA' does in reality.

The furious Scottish club director, desperate to sell Dreyfus because of a Twitter storm he has provoked, is perhaps a little clichéd, but that's forgivable given the restrictions of the format and the need to move the story along quickly. And there are a number of nice touches, notably Dreyfus moaning to his agent that the video game he's playing has underestimated his pace, when he's just 'as fast as Bale or Walcott'. Anti-Thames City graffiti carved into a bench will provide a vital clue.

It's not perfect, but by the standard of TV drama – certainly compared to the dreadful *Endeavour* episode (Season 8, episode 1) based around a death threat received by Oxford Wanderers' star centre-forward – it's pretty good on the detail.

Miss

The Phantom Christmas
(Season 21, episode 6)

A suspect pressed for his whereabouts at 9.36 p.m. 'the night before last' suddenly remembers he was in a pub, the Lord Bassett in Mile End (it does not exist), and that there was football on. The harassed detective, DCI Ben Solomon – played by Elliot Levey, who, curiously, also took on the role of Adam Freedman, a businessman whose wife and son were killed by the same terrorists who went after Isaac Dreyfus in Season 17– snaps that there's football on every night. His suspect recalls it was 'Man U v. Leicester'. It was a 7.45 kick-off, he says, although he admits he wasn't really watching and his friend left shortly before the end. Sure enough, the friend is picked up on the pub's CCTV leaving at 9.27 p.m., providing him with a vital alibi.

But when was this United vs Leicester game? The episode first aired on 23 January 2018. Exactly a month earlier, the sides had indeed met in a 7.45 p.m. kick-off, Harry Maguire scoring a last-minute equaliser for Leicester in a 2–2 draw. But even allowing for the fact that Leicester were at home that day, if this were the game referred to, might not more be made of the fact that DCI Solomon was interviewing his suspect on Christmas Day? And might the weather not be rather colder than it evidently is?

Before that, the previous meeting between Leicester and Manchester United in an evening kick-off came at Old Trafford on 13 April 2004, Gary Neville scoring the only goal. That, though, was an 8 p.m. kick-off, and besides, references to the insurgency in Mali and other elements of the narrative make clear the events are happening at least a decade after that. Given the CCTV backs up the basic timings, the most logical conclusion is that the suspect, who after all was not giving the game his full attention, simply got one or both of the teams wrong. Manchester City, for instance, played Leicester in a 7.45 p.m. kick-off on 4 March 2015.

This, perhaps, is not a mistake but a very realistic detail. People, especially nervous people under pressure, make mistakes.

22.06

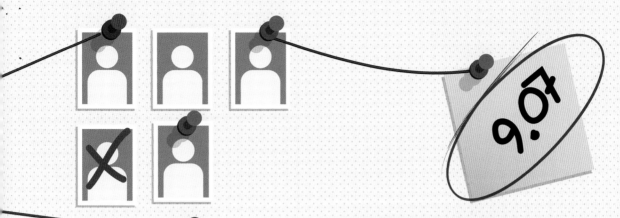

9.07

The Fantasy Spurs Game
(Season 26, episodes 9 and 10)

Two children are in the house when their mother is murdered. The Lyell Centre believes it can establish a timeline of events, as one boy, John, says the other, Ryan, was watching 'the Spurs game' on his phone. This is assumed to have finished at 9.30 p.m. Let's be generous and say that a 7.45 p.m. kick-off would end shortly after 9.30 p.m., even if injury time means it would probably be nearer 9.40 p.m. (the forensic scientists' timings, in this regard, are rather less accurate than they had been in Season 21).

Far more problematic is that we know from the scene in which a suspect is charged that the murder took place on 14 August. We should, therefore, be able to work out which Spurs game Ryan was watching. Spurs played on 14 August in 2022, a 2–2 draw against Chelsea, but that was a Sunday afternoon. They played on 14 August in 2010, a 0–0 draw against Manchester City, but that was a 12.45 p.m. kick-off. Even including friendlies, their last evening kick-off on 14 August was in 2007, a 3–1 home defeat to Everton that kicked off at 8 p.m. – which means it probably ended nearer 10 p.m. than 9.30. But in 2007 it wasn't possible to stream games on a phone, and besides, Ryan has already said his favourite player is Harry Kane, who wouldn't make his Spurs debut until 2011.

So we are left with three possibilities: Ryan was watching a rerun; John was mistaken or has been lied to; or Ryan was not watching football at all. Whichever of those explanations is true, the timeline cannot be relied upon.

The Tell-Tale Badge
(Season 22, episode 3)

After an explosion in a meth lab, the team at the Lyell Centre struggle to identify the badly burned body of a white male in his forties. Dr Thomas Chamberlain observes a 'shield over left pectoral', which, it soon becomes apparent, is from a sports shirt. Closer examination reveals red writing on a yellow field: 'P A R T I Z' and the left half of the letter 'A', which Clarissa Mullery immediately identifies as belonging to the badge of 'FK Partizani, Tirana'. She concludes the victim is Albanian. Dr Nikki Alexander objects that 'he might not be Albanian – he might simply support an Albanian team' and is bemused when Clarissa and Jack Hodgson respond with laughter. 'Why would you do that?' Jack says.

The more famous Partizan, of course, are from Belgrade, but as their colours are black and white, Clarissa's immediate deduction seems reasonable.

9.20

JONATHAN WILSON

JONATHAN LIEW

Full name: Jonathan William Liew
Birthplace: Perivale
Car: Vauxhall Astra

Previous/other clubs/media outlets: Press Association, the *Telegraph*, the *Independent*
Job or trade before becoming a journalist: Sales assistant at Next in Greenford
Nickname: Jonny, Liewandowski
Favourite player: Jonjo Shelvey
A player for the future: Marcus Edwards
Favourite other podcast: *Stadio*
Childhood football hero: Gary Lineker
Favourite other sports: Cricket, darts, tennis, cycling, athletics, snooker, boxing, rugby league, netball (in that order)
Other sportsperson you most admire: Andrea Petkovic
All-time favourite XI: Manuel Neuer; Stephen Carr, David Luiz, Lúcio, Andy Robertson; Jonjo Shelvey, Pedri, Marouane Fellaini; Lionel Messi; Dimitar Berbatov, Vincent Janssen
Most memorable match: Real Madrid 3, Liverpool 1, 2018 Champions League final, Kiev
Biggest disappointment: Netherlands 2, England 0, World Cup qualifier, Rotterdam, 1993
Best stadium visited: Allianz Arena
Favourite food and drink: Ramen, Amaretto Sour
Miscellaneous likes: BBQ Beef Hula Hoops, the 'Deadly'-level Killer Sudoku in *The Times*, marking all my emails as read, even when I haven't read them, the front seat on the top deck of the bus, the Statsguru cricket database
Miscellaneous dislikes: Cars and everything about them
Favourite music: The Thrills
Favourite actor: Humphrey Bogart
Favourite actress: Katharine Hepburn
Favourite holiday destination: Italy
Best film seen recently: *The French Dispatch*
Favourite TV show: *Coupling*
Favourite activity on day off: Instagram
Biggest influence on career: Matthew Syed
Superstitions: I eat noodles for long life every New Year's Eve. It's an old Chinese tradition. Spaghetti is also acceptable. Linguine is a grey area
International honours: A column of mine was once quoted in the Kenyan parliament. It was about twelve years ago. I have no way of proving this
Personal ambition: To reach the end of this sodding questionnaire
If not a journalist, what would you do? Be an academic
Which person in the world would you most like to meet? Bill Bryson

Full name: John Robert Brewin
Birthplace: Taplow, Bucks (I know)
Car: A fourth-hand Mercedes A-class. Sounds flasher than it is; essentially the chosen shopping trolley of the German *Hausfrau* of the mid-2000s
Previous/other clubs/media outlets: ESPN, for longer than I care to remember
Job or trade before becoming a journalist: Worked in a Jobcentre while living in Sheffield: 'Where's me fuckin' giro?' The claims department of a failing insurance company: 'Date of death and policy number, please'

JOHN BREWIN

Favourite player: Zinedine Zidane. I don't give a shit about his xG
A player for the future: James Milner
Favourite other podcast: *Chart Music* and the Fall podcast *Oh! Brother*
Childhood football hero: Bryan Robson. On 1 April 1986, my parents told me he had been sold to Southampton. I sobbed
Other sportsperson you most admire: AP McCoy, Ruby Walsh, Barry Geraghty – the golden generation of jump jockeys
All-time favourite XI: (4–3–3) Alan Zelem; Micky Roberts, Paul McGrath, Alessandro Nesta, Denis Irwin; Bryan Robson, Andrea Pirlo, Zinedine Zidane; Steve Burr, Jonathan Wilkes, Kevin Francis
Most memorable match: Liverpool 3, AC Milan 3, Champions League final, Istanbul, 2005
Best stadium visited: Many of my favourites are gone: Upton Park, the old White Hart Lane, Boothferry Park, Hull.
Favourite food and drink: Fish and chips, by the seaside, with a wooden fork. The odd pint of lager
Miscellaneous likes: Love ginger cats, *Top of the Pops* reruns, fresh air. Morbidly fascinated by the career trajectory of former *Coast* presenter Neil Oliver
Miscellaneous dislikes: Misuse of the word 'narrative', wild accusations of bias from the biased, seeing 'the beautiful game' in articles about football. That I say 'you know' too much. Dogs in pubs
Favourite music: The Fall and the London Boys
Favourite actor: Gary Holton
Favourite actress: Julie Goodyear
Favourite holiday destination: Margate in October
Best film seen recently: *Scum*
Favourite TV show: *The World at War* at Christmas
Favourite activity on day off: Buying records, watching football, pole-vaulting
If not a journalist, what would you do? During the pandemic, I dreamed of being a hard-drinking solicitor in a one-horse town

BREAKING

NEWS

MICHAEL JACKSON IS

DEAD

JOHANNESBURG, 2009. Brazil had just beaten South Africa in the semi-final of the Confederations Cup with a late goal from Dani Alves. I was having a drink in the bar at the Michelangelo Hotel with Duncan White from the *Sunday Telegraph* and Tariq Panja, now of the *New York Times* but then at Bloomberg. Tariq had his laptop open. A news alert pinged. 'Michael Jackson's dead,' he said.

For reasons that remain unclear to me, I turned to the next table, where Gérard Houllier was being interviewed by a group of Japanese journalists. I didn't know Houllier particularly well, but I looked at him and said, 'Gérard, Michael Jackson's dead.' Although the news did send a wave of chatter through the Japanese journalists, he shrugged in a very French way, apparently entirely unconcerned. He may even have said, '*Bof.*'

A couple of minutes later, I went to the gents. On the way, I passed Christian Karembeu, who was returning to his table. I'd never met him before. 'Christian,' I said, 'Michael Jackson's dead.' He shrugged in a very French way, apparently entirely unconcerned. He may even have said, '*Bof.*'

French people, I learned, didn't seem to care much about the death of Michael Jackson. Presented with what felt like one of the biggest news stories of the year, they retained a stereotypical sangfroid.

And that would have been the end of it, had it not been that seven years later, the day after Liverpool lost to Sevilla in the Europa League final, I was speaking at an event in the beautiful Signet Library in Edinburgh. For reasons that escape me, I explained how I'd told Gérard Houllier and Christian Karembeu about the death of Michael Jackson. As I did so, I became aware of a smartly dressed man in the third row, who was bouncing up and down excitedly and waving his hand in the air.

I asked what he wanted.

He stood up. 'My name is Paolo, and I am an Italian sports lawyer,' he said. 'I was also in the bar at the Michelangelo Hotel in Johannesburg that night, sharing a table with Christian Karembeu. At one point, he returned from the toilet and – I never knew until now how he'd found out – but he said to us, "Michael Jackson's dead."'

And that is how news travels.

JONATHAN WILSON

THE FLIES

It says a great deal about the emotional reach, the hard detail of my own contributions to *Guardian Football Weekly* over the last fifteen years that the only thing anyone ever remembers, or will ever remember, is the story of Glenn Hoddle's high-summer turban of flies.

It's not a very good story. In fact, it's not technically a story at all. It has no punchline or narrative arc, just a single haunting central image.

It wasn't even supposed to come up in the first place. I was trying to talk at a live show about the 2018 World Cup in Russia and some interesting details regarding my own family history at the battle of what was then Stalingrad; the impact of visiting the city (now Volgograd) in the company of England fans; the still-visible damage to the topography; the recent drive to rename the city Stalingrad as Russian nationalism began to rise. In the course of which the incidental detail of Glenn Hoddle's high-summer turban of flies, mentioned only in passing, just seemed to grow and spread and fill the skies. Over time there has been a period of slow acceptance. Sometimes you just have to wear that turban of flies. I'm not Antony Beevor. I'm not sweeping warscape reportage. I'm Glenn Hoddle's flypaper hair.

It was very hot in Volgograd, venue for England's opening World Cup group game against Tunisia. I got there two days ahead of time, travelling outside the main England pack as a roving generalist. My grandfather had fought at Stalingrad, on the German side as a Hungarian conscript. He was buried under a pile of rubble – he credited his survival to his fitness: he was also a professional footballer – found by the Russians, allowed to live and shipped off to a labour camp. Presumed dead, he came back to Vienna after the war and, in a cinematic moment, visited his own gravestone.

The modern city was impossibly hot and dusty, a place of harsh climactic extremes. Cue a terrible infestation of flies from the marshy river beds, huge clouds of them following you down the main road into town, creeping inside your face coverings, trying valiantly to go up your nose and into your ears.

It was a sombre time, waiting for the football to happen. Happily, there was one familiar face at my hotel. Glenn Hoddle was there on TV duties. I should add, for the avoidance of doubt, that Glenn has no idea who I am, despite always responding warmly whenever I've said hello to him (which I do, insistently) over the last twenty years of hanging around football. But he was my favourite player growing up, just such a beautifully different, elegant presence.

And here he was again, a courtly, comforting figure, walking the halls, asking for milk at the breakfast buffet, politely negotiating the lobby. When the time came to leave for the game, I found myself waiting for a media bus alone with Glenn, outside in the baking heat. Nothing came. Glenn seemed lost in thought. Finally, he turned to me and said, 'We might have a problem here.'

I tried not to gasp or flinch or scream. His hair was thick with flies. He has always favoured an elevated bouffant, which presumably requires the liberal application of product. I can only assume it was this – Glenn's spray or mousse – that had proved an irresistible draw. The hair itself seemed to be seething, breeding, multiplying. And naturally, I was stunned. Glenn's hair is a monument, a staple, a detail in our shared national infrastructure. It certainly doesn't have flies. Being confronted with this, the only person on earth exposed to this spectacle, felt overwhelming.

I tried raising my hand and brushing it across my hair, trying to mind-nudge Glenn into doing something similar. Instead, he talked a bit about the game and said something about his producer. He stood up to peer around the corner for signs of life, turned back, and I almost screeched. There were, somehow, even more of them, the ratio shifting, a tipping point reached in the balance of hair and insects, whereby flies now vastly outweighed their host body.

And still he remained oblivious. So we sat and talked vaguely, while I stared at the bridge of his nose, until finally the bus appeared and another crisis point arrived. Surely the first person to see Glenn – a colleague, a friend, the driver – would say, 'Oh my god, what have they done to you?'; would round on me, demanding answers; would run inside, calling for an emergency fumigation team.

But Glenn is also a survivor. As the bus pulled to a halt, as I braced for screams and recriminations, he simply raised a hand to his forehead, perhaps sensing something near the hairline, and without noticing sent a vast plume of roosting flies skirling away into the grey summer sky, then stooped to enter the bus, immaculate, hair still sculpted, entirely innocent of the whole affair. We sat through the journey in silence. Glenn never needs to know. He won't remember the incident, nor will he read this (is anyone still reading this?). But it is an image that has buzzed around the *Football Weekly* periphery in the years since, haunting, troubling, but also oddly comforting. And somehow, for reasons that defy rational explanation, being repeated again here.

Barney Ronay

SEVEN AGES of
Football Weekly

EARLY DREAMS

Elis James,
bottom row, third from right,
Prendergast Junior School, 1990

Philippe playing cricket

Max shoots

CRUEL REALITY

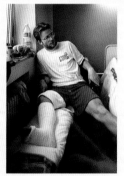

Sid playing

Sid injured

FOREIGN ADVENTURES

Barney plots
escape from
Al Bayt

The landlady of his
guesthouse in Port-Gentil,
Gabon, takes pity on
Nick Ames in 2017, with
the line: 'Le soleil c'est
dangereux pour les
hommes sans cheveux.'

SHOWBIZ ENCOUNTERS !

Jonny
Liew on
Count-
down

Barney and Haddaway
Innsbruck supplementary
media centre, Euro 2008

Barry, Troy and Fiona Bruce

Mark
Langdon,
Hoddle
& Waddle

TIME TO RELAX

AN EXHAUSTING LIFE

Max and Barry

Barry and Wilson share a socially distanced drink on Clapham Common, Christmas 2020

Barry asleep
Max asleep

★ THE RESPECT OF PEOPLE IN THE GAME ★

Lars and Moyes

Lars and Sherwood

Lars and Wenger

Lars and Mourinho

It was September 2015, and a success-starved fanbase was coming round to the idea that a Gareth Bale-inspired Wales team might finally qualify for a major tournament in the post-powdered-egg age. I and 3,500 others had made the trip to Nicosia in Cyprus to watch Wales play one of those fixtures that historically we have found so difficult. A win would leave us three points away from qualification for Euro 2016, our first major tournament in fifty-eight years.

It was an interesting time to be a Wales fan, as received wisdoms about our place in football's pecking order seemed to be changing, so we were all determined to enjoy the match. As I sat in a bar, hours before kick-off, I realised there was free WiFi, which allowed me to check my Twitter. Unbeknown to me, I was on a list somewhere at the BBC in London as 'a Welsh fan who will probably talk to you about football if you ask him', so I saw the following message: 'hi ellis i'm a producer at *world tonight* on bbc radio 4 – are you available later to speak to us about wales leapfrogging eng?' Little old Wales leapfrogging an underpowered, Roy Hodgson-led England team in the FIFA World Rankings. I would love to talk about that, usually. But unfortunately, I was drinking in a cheap beachside bar and trying to keep up with some bigger boys (I was thirty-four at the time). So, a few sheets to the wind, I decided to be uncharacteristically honest with my response, which read: 'I will be shitfaced unfortunately.' Having successfully completed my admin for the day, I put my phone back in my pocket and thought nothing more of it.

←   **Tweet**

Tim Walklate @Walklate88 • 03/09/2015
@elisjames hi ellis i'm a producer at world tonight in bbc radio 4 - are you available later to speak about wales leapfrogging eng?

@Walklate88 I will be shitfaced unfortunately
16:50 · 03/09/2015

My football-hating friend, the comedian Michael Legge, saw this exchange and quote-tweeted it, saying, 'This is the best conversation about sport I have ever seen,' at which point a reply tweeted in haste began to take on a life of its own. In the run-up to kick-off, Michael's tweet started to get serious traction, as my friends and I slurred about possible team selections and whether Aaron Ramsey was better than Ivor Allchurch. Hamstrung by an uncompetitive tariff (despite the speed of my reply to the radio producer, admin isn't actually my strong point), and being a slight miser, I was unwilling to use international data roaming to check my phone, and so had no idea my reply was being seen by more people than I had intended. And besides, with 3,500 Welsh fans expecting a Welsh win, it was party time in Nicosia. I do go on my phone at parties now, but only because I have young children and parties usually happen at soft play.

Wales huffed and puffed on a bumpy pitch against awkward opposition, but Gareth Bale did what Gareth Bale was wont to do and scored a bullet header after 82 minutes, making the difference and bringing us one step closer to qualification. Soft play didn't seem like such a bad idea in the Wales end, as delirious, drunk fans fell over each other, celebrating a goal that would be remembered for years. It was around this time that James Corden saw Michael's tweet and retweeted it to his millions of followers, and suddenly I was trending.

Maybe it was a slow news day, but Welsh newspaper the *Western Mail* thought, 'There's a story in this . . . Tom Jones and Shirley Bassey don't have a record out, and the Welsh bloke who plays the Go.Compare man is no longer returning our calls,' and printed it as a light-hearted companion piece to their coverage of the game. Bizarrely, the *Independent* agreed that my reply was newsworthy and also ran it, with the angle of 'Welsh comedian too pissed to do radio interview'.

It was at this point that a stroke of serendipity helped move things along – again, without my knowledge. I had fallen asleep in a bar in Nicosia, and a friend from school had tweeted a very funny picture, in which I was surrounded by Welsh fans, locals and a couple of curious Belgians who were there for their game a few days later. The news went global, accompanied by the photo. 'Welsh Soccer Fan Too Shitfaced for Interview', screamed news.com.au. 'England might have won The Ashes, but British sports fans are so starved of success they celebrate 1–0 wins against Cyprus by getting shitfaced,' they wrote, employing a typically forgiving Australian attitude to drinking too much lager in the sun.

I found all this out as the seatbelt signs switched off after landing at Heathrow, when I turned on my phone and, to my amazement, saw my Twitter had 1,500 notifications. Initially, I couldn't work out what was happening, as I was dreadfully hungover and my most recent @ messages were at the top. I couldn't understand why so many Australian people I had never met were eager to have a pint with me the next time I was Down Under. As I scrolled through tweet after tweet from accounts in places like Brisbane and Adelaide, each saying things like, 'How's the hangover, YOU RIPPER?!?!?' I couldn't help but notice that I was getting slightly more judgemental tweets from the other side of the Atlantic.

My reply had been covered by the US sports website Deadspin, but the comments beneath the piece were hilarious, as many readers seemed to have misunderstood entirely and assumed I was a *player*. 'He's nothing but a Western European binge drinker,' said one. 'I think it's unprofessional that you get drunk before a game,' said another. Why? 'Oh,' I realised. 'This guy from Texas seems to think that I've had seven pints and a Jägerbomb before lining up alongside Ashley Williams and Ben Davies in a crucial European Championship qualifier.'

It was a slightly odd week. We played Israel at home three days later, and walking into pubs in Cardiff to be welcomed by slaps on the back from strangers felt like I had given everyone in Wales access to my teenage diary or had had to sit on the toilet in front of the Stretford End at Old Trafford. My agent at the time was delighted: 'You're carving out a great niche for yourself!'

I'd like to think that I am now known as a deeply handsome (yet relatable) radio presenter, as opposed to a pissed bloke who can't handle his beer. But it's very difficult to control your own legacy.

The
Low Performance
PODCAST

Do you have no A-levels but would like to own an Aga?

Do you have responsibilities like a hefty mortgage and a family to feed?

Do you want to embark on a new career you know nothing about?

WATCH NOW   LISTEN NOW

If you answered 'yes', 'yes' and 'yes', then have we got the niche podcast for you!

It doesn't matter in which field of endeavour our guests have failed – sport, music, business, art, entertainment, the fast-food industry – they all have first-hand experiences and lessons learned the hard way, and they're ready to share. They'll cover the full gamut, from divorce, bankruptcy, alcoholism and drug abuse to supervised fortnightly visiting rights and public shame.

On the *Low Performance Podcast* we find out what non-negotiable behaviours our guests should have employed to get them to the top, only for them to embrace different, detrimental ones. We also ask them what motivational hokum from Norfolk-based self-styled life-coaching gurus they really wish they'd ignored. We can all learn from their failures and choose to sit on the easy chair.

On *Low Performance*, we turn the lived experiences of the planet's most high-profile failures into your cautionary tales.

PHILIPPE AUCLAIR

ARCHIE RHIND-TUTT

Full name: Archie Maurice Rhind-Tutt
Birthplace: London
Previous/other clubs/media outlets: LBC
Job or trade before becoming a journalist: Work experience as a Costa Coffee barista. Dropped cups. Despite verbal agreement, contract offer was rescinded

Favourite player: Jeremie Frimpong
A player for the future: Randal Kolo Muani
Favourite other podcast: *The Bugle*
Childhood football hero: Brian McBride
Favourite other sports: Test cricket, tennis, ski cross
Other sportsperson you most admire: Andy Murray
All-time favourite XI: Edwin van der Sar; Steve Finnan, Brede Hangeland, Tim Ream, Rufus Brevett; Steed Malbranque, Sylvain Legwinski, Steed Malbranque, Luís Boa Morte; Brian McBride, Louis Saha
Most memorable match: Aston Villa 0, Fulham 1, Championship play-off final, Wembley, 2018.
Biggest disappointment: Diego Forlán breaking my heart in Hamburg
Best stadium visited: SC Freiburg's (old) Schwarzwald Stadion
Favourite food and drink: Welsh cakes and Fritz-Limo lemonade
Miscellaneous likes: Ping-pong, Tetris, Pac-Man, water slides, Yoga with Adrienne, playing the keyboard, Fortuna Köln
Miscellaneous dislikes: People who refer to themselves in the third person, metal hangers, liquorice, gin
Favourite music: ELO, Haim, Robyn
Favourite actor: Steve Carell
Favourite actress: Chelsea Peretti
Favourite holiday destination: Lukas Podolski's kebab shop
Best film seen recently: *Airplane*
Favourite TV show: *The Office* (US)
Favourite activity on day off: Tetris
Biggest influence on career: Derek Rae
Superstitions: Once believing that by praying every time the opposition entered the Fulham half, it would prevent them from scoring.
International honours: Witness to Fulham's Intertoto Cup triumph of 2002
Personal ambition: To play 'Great Balls of Fire' on the keyboard
If not a journalist, what would you do? Be the Fortuna Köln mascot, Fred the red panda

Full name: Philippe Jean-Hervé François Auclair
Birthplace: Yvetot, France
Car: None; I don't have a driving licence
Previous/other clubs/media outlets: Too many to mention, but very proud of being the first Frenchman to be published in *Wisden* and *The Cricketer*
Job or trade before becoming a journalist: Teacher, fruit picker, chef, board games creator, mushroom forager, musician, sound recordist for wildlife documentaries, translator, voice-over artist
Nickname: Fifi (not 'Phil', please)
Favourite player: Dennis Bergkamp
A player for the future: Rayan Cherki. Possibly
Favourite other podcast: *The Rest Is History*
Childhood football hero: George Best
Favourite other sports: Cycling and cricket
Other sportsperson you most admire: Julian Alaphilippe
All-time favourite XI: Lev Yashin; Cafu, Marius Trésor, Ruud Gullit, Manuel Amoros; Jean Tigana, Patrick Vieira; Flórián Albert, Dennis Bergkamp, Roger Magnusson; Brazilian Ronaldo
Most memorable match: France 3, West Germany 3, World Cup semi-final, Sevilla, 1982
Biggest disappointment: In football? Arsenal vs Barcelona, Champions League final, 2006
Best stadium visited: Craven Cottage
Favourite food and drink: Belon oysters and Meursault
Miscellaneous likes: Chess, puzzles, mushrooms, hiking, snorkelling, Alexandre Dumas, Flann O'Brien, Jun'ichirō Tanizaki, Philip Larkin, Yōko Ogawa, long train journeys
Miscellaneous dislikes: Flying, hotel breakfasts, Ed Sheeran, Nike ads, Harald Schumacher, FIFA
Favourite music: Ravel's *L'enfant et les sortilèges*
Favourite actor: Roger Livesey
Favourite actress: Veronica Lake
Favourite holiday destination: Mexico
Best film seen recently: *Drive My Car*
Favourite TV show: *Mad Men*
Favourite activity on day off: Mushroom hunting
Biggest influence on career: Brian Glanville
Superstitions: None
International honours: Er …
Personal ambition: To outlive Gianni Infantino
If not a journalist, what would you do? Music, music and more music
Which person in the world would you most like to meet? Given a chance to travel back in time, Orson Welles

BEYONCÉ IN THE DONBAS

IT WAS AUGUST 2009. At first, it seemed I couldn't go to the official opening of the Donbas Arena, to which I'd inexplicably been invited. It fell the day after a friend's wedding, as I regretfully explained to the organisers. To which they replied, slightly sinisterly, that they would send a car to pick me up at 4 a.m. on the day of the event, and I could then fly to Vienna and catch a connection to Donetsk. Although I'd miss the lunch, I'd be there comfortably in time for the main event. I had no idea how they knew where I lived.

The ceremony was, as far as these things go, pretty good. There was a speech from Viktor Yanukovych (who, five years later, would be deposed as Ukrainian president after the Euromaidan protests), which was interesting in a number of ways, and a bizarre passage in which Shakhtar's youth side played five-a-side against a team of mechanical spiders. Then came the main event: a concert for which Beyoncé had been flown in from Tokyo at a cost of $25 million.

I'm no great fan of music or loud noise, so, after five minutes or so, with the wedding hangover still throbbing away, I went off to find some booze. A couple of floors down, I found a free champagne bar, which was largely populated by former Shakhtar players. After an enjoyable hour or so, I realised Beyoncé had finished and I should probably shuffle off and do what I was there for.

The journalists had been invited to a 'mixed zone-style event', at which we could talk to the stadium architect, the local mayor and other vaguely relevant officials. In football, the mixed zone is the space between the dressing rooms and the team buses where journalists stand in a long line on one side of a barrier while players walk past on the other, occasionally stopping for a quick interview. The problem was, nobody had said where this was happening, so I followed the signs for 'Mixed Zone'. It turned out, though, that this mixed zone was happening not in the official mixed zone near the dressing rooms but outside on the steps, so as I got deeper and deeper into the bowels of the stadium, I was moving further and further from where I was supposed to be.

I realised I'd gone wrong when I found myself in a lift with Jádson, Ilsinho and Luiz Adriano and their respective partners, but by then it was too late. Booze and fatigue blurring the edges, I staggered on into a crowded corridor. Seeing a sign for the mixed zone, I optimistically got out my Dictaphone. And then, suddenly, a yard in front of me, there was Beyoncé.

'Errr, what do you think of the stadium?' I blurted out, thrusting the Dictaphone in her face.

Confusion flickered momentarily in her eyes. 'It's a lovely place you've got here,' she said. That left me befuddled. Did she think . . .? 'Oh no,' I said, 'it's not mine . . .'

At which security whisked me away. Beyoncé, I learned, is surprisingly tall.

JONATHAN WILSON

SAM ALLARDYCE | PER FRANDSEN | SAMMY LEE | KEVIN NOLAN AND JAY-JAY OKOCHA

They're having so much fun it's illegal.

OH, SAM'S XI

BOLTON WANDERERS PRESENTS

In Association with PREMIER LEAGUE PICTURES and UEFA CUP ENTERTAINMENT, a SAM ALLARDYCE/SAMMY LEE production starring in alphabetical order
SAM ALLARDYCE PER FRANDSEN SAMMY LEE KEVIN NOLAN and JAY-JAY OKOCHA
'Oh, Sam's XI' EL HADJI DIOUF, YOURI DJORKAEFF, PER FRANDSEN, RICARDO GARDNER, STELIOS GIANNAKOPOULOS, JUSSI JÄÄSKELAINEN
Costume Design by REEBOK Edited by IVAN CAMPO Production Designer FERNANDO HIERRO Music by HENRIK PEDERSEN Co-Produced NICKY HUNT
Executive Producers NICOLAS ANELKA MIKE WHITLOW and TAL BEN HAIM
Screenplay by SAM ALLARDYCE Produced by PHIL GARTSIDE Directed by SAM ALLARDYCE

Deception, Back-Stabbing and Lake Como: An Oral History

**The break-up and rebirth of *Football Weekly*.
As told by the people themselves***

Barry Glendenning: In late July 2017, around the time the first *Football Weekly* podcast of the 2017–18 season was due to be recorded, I sent an email to James Richardson and Producer Ben reminding them that the Community Shield between Arsenal and Chelsea was imminent and we should probably get the collective finger out and assemble in the studio to record our big pre-season show.

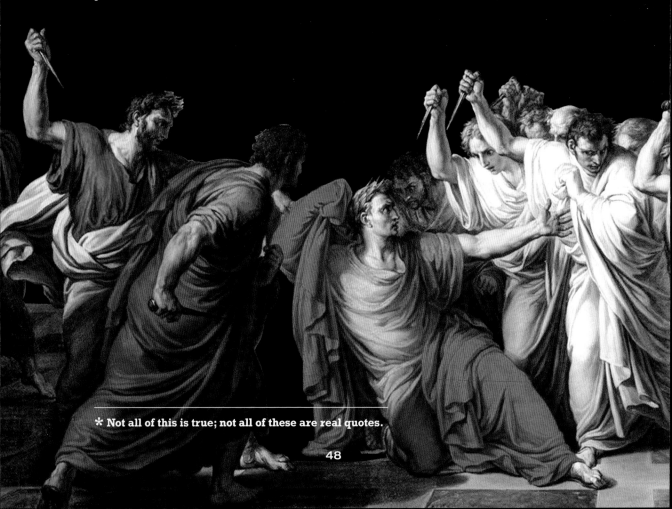

***** Not all of this is true; not all of these are real quotes.

While my recollection is a little sketchy, I remember being eager to get my predictions for the new campaign down on tape for the record: Manchester City to win the title, with Swansea, Stoke and West Brom going down. While it's not really pertinent to the story, I also forecast Chelsea to win the FA Cup, City to lift the first of four consecutive League Cups and Real Madrid to win the Champions League.

Neither Jimbo nor Ben replied, so a day or two later, I followed up with WhatsApp messages. They didn't reply to those either, even though the blue ticks proved the messages had been read. The whiff of what can only be described as rat in the air was as palpable as it was overpowering.

James Richardson: I remember it like it was yesterday. Matters came to a head when the *Guardian* bosses tried to impose a word-play limit on my script. That was one pun-ishment I wasn't willing to take. [*Wry look to camera.*]

Iain Macintosh: It was late one night. I'd just taken Altrincham into the Premier League in my eighteenth season in FM2017, and I idly wondered if I could single-handedly tear apart the world's most successful football podcast. I started whispering to Jimbo that if we played our cards right, we could launch a very similar pod, just without the shackles of the tofu-eating wokerati *Guardian* editorial constraints. And with way more gambling advertising.

JR: And we'd get to talk about fantasy football. And there's nothing people like to hear about more than fantasy football teams that aren't theirs.

Producer Ben: My book *Podcast Master* is a complete bargain on Kindle these days. Your one-stop shop for learning how to make a successful podcast, like I used to do.

Producer Joel: I was producing *606* on Radio 5 Live. I didn't turn up at *Football Weekly* until four years later. My input really isn't needed, but I do like to stick my oar in from time to time.

BG: A few days after having my correspondence to Jimbo and Producer Ben ignored, I finally received a phone call from soon-to-be former friend of the show Iain Macintosh. He told me that he, James, Ben and others were going rogue and splitting from the *Guardian* to set up their own version of *Football Weekly*. He explained that apart from having the exact same presenter and many of the exact same guests discussing the exact same things, it would be completely different to *Football Weekly*. He also told me that there was a chance it might still be called *Football Weekly*, because they were hoping to sell it back to the *Guardian*, which they presumed would be desperate not to lose its flagship podcast.

As I was standing in the beer garden of my local pub and completely pissed at the time, I couldn't really remember much of the conversation, and only discovered the full gravity of what was going on when I sobered up, rang Macintosh back the next day and asked him to explain it all to me again. I would later discover that, in fact, I was not part of their plans. I subsequently called James Richardson and told him he had until 6 p.m. to inform the *Guardian* bosses himself or else I'd do it. A few hours later, I grassed him and his cronies up. To say the *Guardian* higher-ups were stunned would be an understatement..

JR: You could say it was complete Macin-tosh. [*Wry look to camera.*]

BG: I rang Max to tell him what was going on. Along with the Current Mrs Rushden, he was on Lake Como. Of course he was.

Max Rushden: I was on holiday with the Current Mrs Rushden. We were sunning ourselves on the shores of Lake Como when the phone rang. It was Barry. He never calls me in the daytime. And when he calls me after 8 p.m., I don't pick up.

The Current Mrs Rushden: Every time we're on holiday, Max gets some stupid call about some job or other, and then he's just on his phone. Sky . . . blah, blah, blah . . . talkSPORT . . . blah, blah, blah . . . the *Guardian* . . . blah, blah. Well, not so much Sky any more.

MR: We were in Varenna, in a tiny Airbnb hosted by a three-hundred-year-old Italian woman who insisted on cooking frozen pizzas for us every time we got back

to the apartment. Barry explained the *Football Weekly* situation, saying to me: 'If you don't get this job, then you really are shit.' I'd done the podcast before; I'd even brought Trevor Nelson's microwave to the Palladium for a live-show gag. Although I've been a shoo-in for jobs before and haven't got them, so I didn't count any chickens.

Jonathan Wilson: I'd just left the library in Szombathely, in western Hungary, where I'd been having coffee with the man who used to dry-clean Ferenc Puskás's accountant's nephew's suits, interviewing him for a book I was writing that no one would read. I got a text from Miguel Delaney, from the *Indy*, which I assumed would be about the terrible WiFi in the press box at Old Trafford. Turned out he was actually moaning about a train he was about to board being cancelled, and some agent had told him about a signing Villa were about to make, and a human rights group had been on to him about something or other, and somebody else was an awful twat. Oh yes, he'd also heard that Jimbo had walked.

Jordan Jarrett-Bryan: Maybe it's me, I don't know. But, I mean, what does the sky do? It's got to do better than that, for me. I just don't know what it's supposed to be.

Nedum Onuoha: I was in Salt Lake City trying to become a Mormon.

(**Jürgen Klopp:** Have you ever actually played the game?

NO: Welllllllllll . . .)

BG: It was around this time that Daniel Storey broke the news on *Football 365* that James Richardson was leaving *Football Weekly*, and all hell broke loose on the internet as it was the biggest story of the transfer window. I'm not sure how Daniel got this scoop, but I'm told he is now a regular guest on *The Totally Football Show*, which you can find on the sports podcast charts if you have time to scroll down far enough.

Gianni Infantino: Today, I feel Barry.

MR: Someone rang from the *Guardian* and asked if I'd host the next few pods because Jimbo couldn't make it. They didn't know that I knew. So I asked what was up – because under the old regime I'd always been given months of notice if Jimbo was going to be off. I asked with such authority that their cover broke and they explained what Baz had already explained. So I said I wanted the gig, permanently – and they said OK. After I'd signed the contract, William Hill still had me at 7/4 to get the gig. But I didn't put any money on because I'm a massive square, didn't know if it was legal and had no desire to go to prison.

Dave Farrar: I was 7/1. But no one called me.

JJB: Is it night, is it day? Is it blue, is it grey? You never know, do you? Sun, rain, snow, fog. It's just not consistent enough.

JW: A lot of people think of the early 1950s as the golden age of Hungarian football, but actually the *Aranycsapat* was the final flowering of a fecund culture stretching back, I think you could argue, to 1916, when Jimmy Hogan, having been interned in Vienna, was spirited out of house arrest to move to Budapest and coach MTK.

Sid Lowe: I was on a train with a shit signal talking to Jimbo about Toni Kroos when the line went dead. The next thing I know, the phone's ringing and it's that twat from *Soccer AM*. No, not Tim Lovejoy, the other one.

Julien Laurens: GOOOOAAAAAL FOOOOR PSG!

John Brewin: I was at home ranking Lighthouse Family singles when I saw the news. I raised an eyebrow and went back to the job in hand. 'Lifted' over 'Ocean Drive' for me, Clive.

IM: I bought a drinks globe like a top mogul and started playing *Civilization IV* for money.

51

JG. With speculation rampant on Twitter and in media circles that *Football Weekly* was completely fucked, we were desperate to get our first podcast of the season out before 'them'. We rustled up a panel of loyal guests whose heads hadn't been turned, and I think Max might have been forced to cut his Italian holiday short. It's testament to the Current Mrs Rushden's patience that he was allowed to do so.

Lars Sivertsen: I put down my breakfast. The lamb dhansak had seen better days anyway. I gave Lola a saveloy and shut the front door. Since I'd never done the pod and didn't know anyone involved in the whole thing, no one rang. But that's OK.

Barney Ronay: It was just like that Philip Larkin poem.

Niccolo Machiavelli: Politics have no relation to morals.

Pep Guardiola: Guys, guys . . . this guy . . . oh my god, this guy . . . so good, so good.

JW: I was on the bus home after seeing my financial adviser when Producer Iain called and asked if I could do the next *Football Weekly*. Then he asked me to do the one after that. And also the fee had more than doubled. I'd been on only twice the previous year, as they sidelined those with other *Guardian* connections before the split, so I knew things were changing.

Producer Iain: It wasn't me. Maybe you're thinking of Shadowy Uber-producer Jason?

Shadowy Uber-producer Jason: I still have mild heart palpitations when I recollect that particular event, partly because the whole thing scuppered my sabbatical and I missed my sister's fiftieth birthday.

Matt Le Tissier: This hat? Tin foil.

JJB: Look, I've nothing against the sky per se; it's just, what's it actually for? What does it do?

Troy Townsend: To be perfectly honest with you, I'd never heard of anybody involved, so I asked Andros. He didn't know any of them either.

BR: It was also very much like a pipe-smoking anthropomorphised badger in Victorian garb doing something unlikely.

David Mellor: It all felt like a blow for those of us who just loved red-hot soccer chat.

Elis James: Oh, man. [*Exhales deeply.*] Let me tell you about Gareth Bale. Gareth. Bale. This man. What he has done for me. Oh, Gareth. I can't articulate it in a way that will give it the meaning it deserves. But at his peak, and granted I didn't get to see John Charles, but at his peak, well – and I know Giggs and Hughes and that generation. But Gareth Bale. He is the greatest I ever saw. I could just watch him run until my dying breath and I'd be happy. He cares about Wales. He has no idea what he's done for me. He's like a father, a brother and a son all at the same time. I love him.

James Horncastle: Which what? Oh, Timotei.

BG: We recorded the first episode of the new era, sent it out into the ether and the response was . . . mixed. It would be fair to say that Max was not, and still isn't, everyone's cup of tea.

MR: I remember the first episode. We spent a lot of time on in-jokes about the changes – which in retrospect wasn't the wisest thing, given that a lot of listeners aren't on social media and had no idea what had happened until they heard my voice and a virtually new panel. Some people obviously hated it – someone called me a 'banter boy'.

NM: Men should be treated either generously or destroyed, because they take revenge for slight injuries – for heavy ones they cannot.

Eddie Howe: I'm just a football guy. I'm just here to talk about football.

Philippe Auclair: I am one of the few people to appear on both podcasts. Then I had a nice chat on the phone with Max, and I chose wisely.

NM: If an injury has to be done to a man, it should be so severe that his vengeance need not be feared.

BG: The naysayers were vocal on social media, and while it would have been nice to mention their doom-mongering when collecting our FSA award for best podcast in a ceremony hosted by James Richardson under the shadow of Traitors' Gate at the Tower of London several months later, I thought that to do so might have been considered churlish. Instead, I chose as inspiration Father Ted Crilly's infamous speech at the Golden Cleric Awards, which seemed to go down a storm. 'And now, the liars . . .'

Jake Humphrey: I mean, the weirdest thing is that all this happened several years before I'd even invented the podcast, an aural medium many people warned me was too niche. And I didn't get any A-levels, but I do have a social conscience, a Range Rover and an Aga.

Click here to subscribe →

Full name: Chinedum Onuoha
Birthplace: Ovwian Aladja, Nigeria
Car: Mini Countryman Hybrid
Previous/other clubs/media outlets: ESPN, BBC
Job or trade before becoming a journalist: Footballer
Nickname: Chief

NEDUM ONUOHA

A player for the future: Bukayo Saka
Favourite other podcast: *Pardon My Take*
Childhood football hero: Thierry Henry
Favourite other sports: Athletics
Other sportsperson you most admire: Usain Bolt
All-time favourite XI: Manuel Neuer; Cafu, Gerard Piqué, Sergio Ramos, Philipp Lahm; Xavi, Patrick Vieira, Andrés Iniesta; Lionel Messi, Ronaldo, Ronaldinho
Most memorable match: Argentina 3, France 3, 2022 World Cup final, Lusail Stadium, Qatar
Biggest disappointment: QPR in the Premier League
Best stadium visited: Camp Nou
Favourite food and drink: Anything Nigerian
Miscellaneous likes: Travelling the world
Miscellaneous dislikes: Having my time wasted
Favourite music: Hip hop, Afrobeats
Favourite actor: Denzel Washington, Leonardo DiCaprio
Favourite actress: Jessica Chastain, Emily Blunt
Favourite holiday destination: USA
Best film seen recently: *Matilda the Musical*
Favourite TV show: More of a YouTube guy
Favourite activity on day off: Brunching
Biggest influence on career: My family
Superstitions: Don't be superstitious but let others be if they need it
International honours: 2009 UEFA European Under-21 Championship runner-up
Personal ambition: Don't work so hard that it appears I'm no longer retired
If not a pundit, what would you do? Likely nothing and be free as a bird
Which person in the world would you most like to meet? Usain Bolt

SID LOWE

Full name: Dr Simon (Sid) James Lowe
Birthplace: Whittington Hospital, Norf London. Just like Laurie Cunningham
Previous/other clubs/media outlets: Grisú CF, Southgate Olympic, *The Spanish Football Podcast*, ESPN, *World Soccer*
Job or trade before becoming a journalist: Teaching southern European fascism at Barnsley College. Although none of them actually became fascists
Nickname: None that stuck. Briefly there was a Le Tissier-based one, which doesn't seem so good now
A player for the future: Nico Williams. The Basque one, not the Welsh one
Favourite other podcast: *The Spanish Football Podcast*
Childhood football hero: Kenny Dalglish
Favourite other sports: When I went to the Olympics, the unexpected revelation was weightlifting
Other sportsperson you most admire: As a kid, it was Boris Becker. These don't always age well, do they?
All-time favourite XI: A maverick selection of fourteen players who don't in any sense form a team: Esteban, Abel Xavier, Diego Cervero, Kenny Dalglish, Juan Mata, Iñaki Williams, Diego Maradona, John Barnes, Matt Le Tissier, Petr Dubovský, Miguel Linares, Santi Cazorla, Michu, Original Ronaldo
Most memorable match: Liverpool 3, Everton 1, 1986 FA Cup final
Biggest disappointment: Real Oviedo getting relegated from the Primera División at Mallorca in 2001, which turned out to be even worse than it seemed at the time
Best stadium visited: The old San Mamés
Favourite food and drink: *Dulce de leche*, tea
Miscellaneous likes: Spanish water dogs
Miscellaneous dislikes: I don't know how many fire hydrants there are, I can't remember my password and, no, I don't want to register, you bastards. Printers
Favourite music: Whatever the *guaje* is playing and 'Bad Moon Rising', which he won't be
Favourite actor: Rik Mayall
Favourite actress: Carrie Fisher
Favourite holiday destination: Cadiz
Best film seen recently: *Sonic the Hedgehog*
Favourite TV show: *The Young Ones*
Favourite activity on day off: On what?
Biggest influence on career: Tea
Superstitions: Always put your pants on before your trousers
International honours: More than a hundred Spanish cups
Personal ambition: A fully functioning ankle
If not a journalist, what would you do? A proper job
Which person in the world would you most like to meet? Maradona and Mandela. Alas, a bit late for that

THE OUT-OF-season, seasonal QUIZ

1
Fill in the gap:
Roy Hodgson, Steve Clarke, Keith Downing, Pepe Mel, ____ ____, Rob Kelly, Tony Pulis, Gary Megson, Alan Pardew.

2
Who, having played in all seven of Everton's ties in the 1984 FA Cup, scoring against Stoke in the third round and Shrewsbury in the fifth, was left out of the match-day squad for the final?

3
Which coach, who brought through the likes of Peter Ramage and Steven Taylor as academy director at Blackburn and Newcastle, was described by Damien Duff as the best he'd ever worked with?

4
Who was manager of Preston North End when they lost to Sheffield United in the Championship play-off semi-final in 2008–9?

5
Which winger, a boyhood fan of Eddie Gray who studied to be an insurance broker while playing for Queen's Park, played 109 games for Crystal Palace between 1984 and 1987?

6
Who was temporary manager of Norwich City between the dismissal of Alex Neil in March 2017 and the appointment of Daniel Farke two months later?

ANSWERS:

Alan Irvine. 2. Alan Irvine. 3. Alan Irvine. 4. Alan Irvine. 5. Alan Irvine. 6. Alan Irvine

MY BEST SHOTS

Tom Jenkins has been a sports photographer at the *Guardian* for more than three decades. Here he selects his favourite action shots.

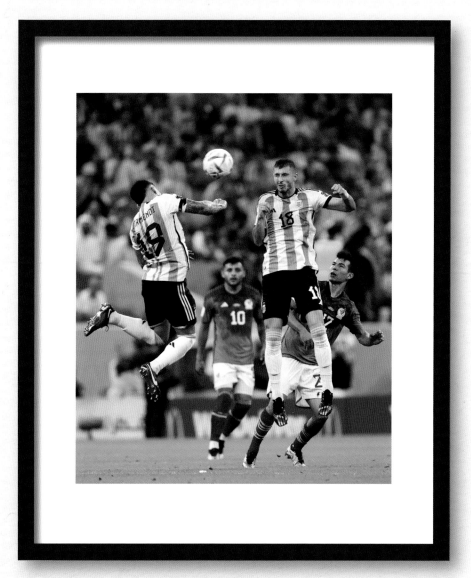

Nicolás Otamendi and Guido Rodríguez jump for the ball as Alexis Vega and Hirving Lozano look on during Argentina's 2–0 group-stage win over Mexico at the Lusail Stadium in the 2022 World Cup.

Newcastle's Shay Given saves a shot from Manchester United's Gary Pallister during their 1–1 draw at Old Trafford in April 1998.

Júlio Baptista and Michael Essien collide during Chelsea's win over Arsenal in the 2007 League Cup final at the Millennium Stadium in Cardiff.

Rob Jones of Sheffield Wednesday wins a header against Richard Cresswell of Sheffield United in a League One match at Bramall Lane, October 2011.

Roger Espinoza beats Joan Capdevila to hook the ball on in Honduras's 2–0 defeat to Spain at Ellis Park in the 2010 World Cup.

Raúl Jiménez beats Aaron Ramsdale to put Wolves a goal up in their 2–0 win at Sheffield United on the opening day of the season, September 2020.

José Mourinho keeps the ball from Steven Gerrard during the infamous 'slip' match in which Chelsea beat Liverpool at Anfield, April 2014.

Mateja Kežman gets Chelsea's third in their victory over Liverpool in the 2005 League Cup final in Cardiff.

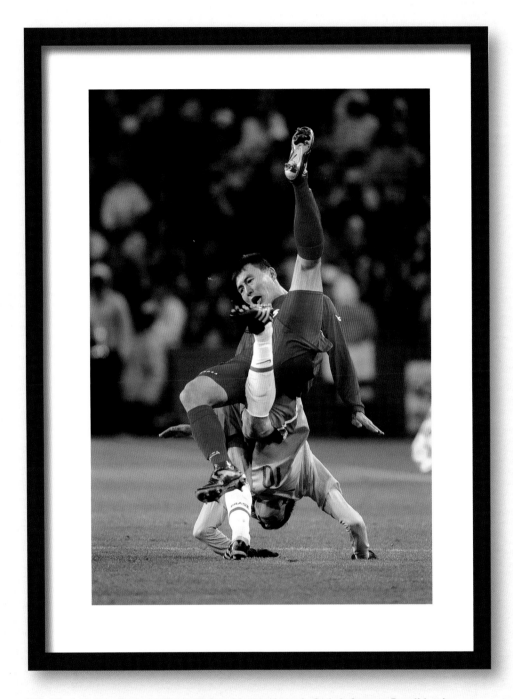

Pak Chol-Jin challenges Kaká during North Korea's 2–1 defeat to Brazil in the group stage of the 2010 World Cup at Ellis Park, Johannesburg.

Israel's Yoav Ziv slides in on Shaun Wright-Phillips during England's 3–0 win over Israel in a Euro 2008 qualifier at Wembley, September 2007.

Eduardo Vargas's header slithers between Simon Mignolet and Rhian Brewster as QPR lose 3–2 to Liverpool in October 2019.

The Spurs keeper Heurelho Gomes stretches desperately for the ball, but the goal is given as Frank Lampard puts Chelsea ahead in their April 2011 Premier League clash.

Manuel Almunia can't stop James McFadden's free kick as Arsenal draw 2–2 at Birmingham City in February 2008.

Efe Sodje wins a header in front of Rio Ferdinand during Nigeria's 0–0 draw against England in Osaka at the 2002 World Cup.

Petr Čech claims a cross during Chelsea's 2–1 win over Arsenal at the Emirates Stadium, September 2012.

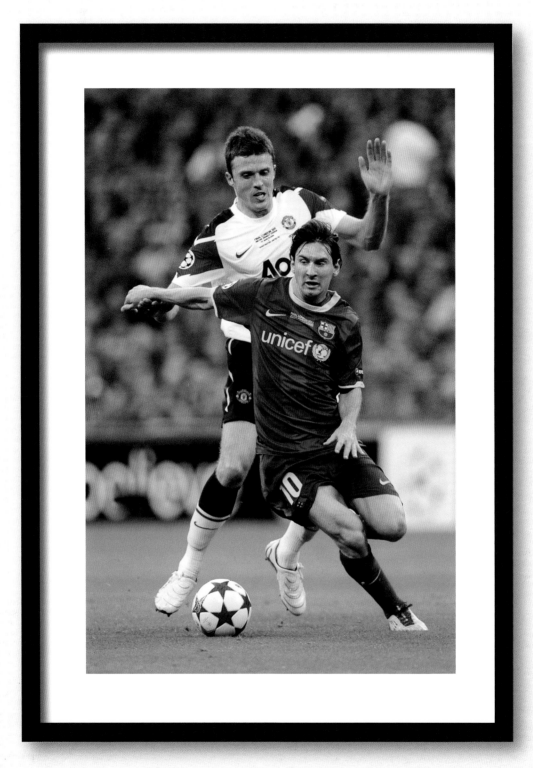

Lionel Messi gets away from Michael Carrick as Barcelona beat Manchester United 3–1 in the 2011 Champions League final at Wembley.

LEAGUE CUP FINAL WORD SEARCH!

The grid below contains the names of all twenty-four Manchester City and Newcastle United players who played a part in the 1976 League Cup final. When you've found all their names, enjoy the secret message hidden in the rest of the grid.

T	H	O	T	A	L	I	T	A	R	I	A	S	N	H	O
G	O	W	L	I	N	G	M	O	P	H	S	N	O	B	I
C	W	B	O	O	T	H	M	I	S	A	O	R	G	Y	N
I	A	A	H	A	R	T	F	O	R	D	S	U	S	T	Y
S	R	R	P	O	K	U	R	T	T	S	W	B	T	A	D
S	D	R	H	I	N	E	T	G	H	U	M	A	N	A	E
N	R	O	I	G	C	A	S	S	I	D	Y	R	E	C	N
M	H	W	T	S	N	R	A	B	U	S	I	N	M	A	N
A	N	C	D	G	T	T	A	O	R	M	N	E	E	N	E
C	T	L	O	U	R	E	D	I	E	A	T	S	L	N	K
D	R	O	Y	L	E	E	N	T	G	H	I	O	C	E	N
O	W	U	L	I	T	H	O	I	U	O	T	T	E	L	R
N	A	G	E	E	K	I	R	A	L	N	A	L	B	L	S
A	O	H	L	U	T	R	E	M	O	E	E	N	A	R	C
L	H	Y	S	N	O	S	T	A	W	Y	H	A	M	E	M
D	O	N	A	C	H	I	E	U	R	D	E	R	O	U	S

Corrigan	Barnes	Mahoney	Burns
Keegan	Booth	Nattrass	Cassidy
Donachie	Royle	Kennedy	Macdonald
Doyle	Hartford	Barrowclough	Gowling
Watson	Tueart	Keeley	Craig
Oakes	Clements	Howard	Cannell

_____ vs _____

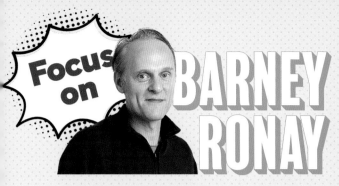

Full name: Barnaby Vincent Ronay
Birthplace: London
Car: Ice-blue Ford Sierra Cosworth
Previous/other clubs/media outlets: *When Saturday Comes*, *The Cricketer*
Job or trade before becoming a journalist: Parliamentary agent
Nickname: Beavis
Favourite player: Paul Gascoigne
A player for the future: Fodé Ballo-Touré
Favourite other podcast: *The Grade Cricketer*
Childhood football hero: Terry Hurlock
Favourite other sports: Cricket, fives, real tennis, rackets, fencing, shooting
Other sportsperson you most admire: Shelly-Ann Fraser-Pryce
All-time favourite XI: The Denmark team that won Euro '92 is the team I'd most like to have been a part of. It looked fun. They beat some serious teams. I'd like to be friends with Flemming Povlsen
Most memorable match: None
Biggest disappointment: Jan Vennegoor of Hesselink
Best stadium visited: Lusail Iconic Stadium. How many other grounds are officially iconic? I can think of none
Favourite food and drink: Steak, lager, prawn cocktail, Black Forest gateau
Miscellaneous dislikes: Rude people, washing the car, the boundless daily ennui of the quotidian existence, disco music
Favourite music: Lionel Richie
Favourite actor: Al Pacino
Favourite actress: Raquel Welch
Favourite holiday destination: Never happier than when I'm yomping up a Munro
Best film seen recently: *Liquorice Pizza*
Favourite TV show: Anything on beIN Sports
Favourite activity on day off: Uneasiness
Biggest influence on career: Fear, money and lack of bold entrepreneurial initiative. The Ring Lardner book *You Know Me Al*
Superstitions: Ascetic Lutheranism
International honours: Qualified to play for England, Germany, Austria, Hungary and India
Personal ambition: None. All my ambitions are for other people. Currently, I want Jonathan Wilson to win the Thunderball lottery and buy a personalised working replica steam train
If not a journalist, what would you do? Impertinent
Which person in the world would you most like to meet? Evel Knievel, Alan Shearer and Lytton Strachey, combined into a single person, but with horse-like legs

Full name: Nicky Bandini
Birthplace: London
Car: As if! I grew up in London
Previous/other clubs/media outlets: I'm a freelancer, so I'm all over the place, but of course the big one was being the *first-ever* head of sport for Warwick University's student-run TV society – a position I won by promising a great number of things that were beyond my capabilities. We did not, in the end, broadcast the university table tennis club's games live to the student union bar

Job or trade before becoming a journalist: Lots! But the best fun was flipping patties at Roxy Burger in downtown Vancouver
Nickname: Tree
Favourite player: Bukayo Saka
A player for the future: Haley Bugeja
Favourite other podcast: Obviously, the one I make with Mina Rzouki, *Serie A Chronicles*. But also *The Magnus Archives*
Childhood football hero: Walter Zenga! I remember very little of the 1990 World Cup, but I know I got very protective of him when all the adults were blaming him for things going wrong. I asked for his replica shirt that Christmas, though with hindsight I'm fairly sure Mum just gave me a goalkeeping shirt she found and told me that was the one!
Favourite other sports: American football, tennis, competitive eating
All-time favourite XI: Gigi Buffon; Gianluca Zambrotta, Fabio Cannavaro, Marco Materazzi, Fabio Grosso; Mauro Camoranesi, Gennaro Gattuso, Andrea Pirlo, Simone Perrotta; Francesco Totti, Luca Toni. Off the bench: Daniele De Rossi, Vincenzo Iaquinta, Alessandro Del Piero. Manager: Marcello Lippi. Opponents: France
Biggest disappointment: I want to say something light-hearted and fun like 'Emirates Stadium pizza', but the real answer right now is how easily people who claimed to want to make a gesture of solidarity with LGBTQ+ people in Qatar capitulated at the first hint of personal risk
Best stadium visited: San Siro will always be the place that gives me goosebumps. Steer clear of the loos, though, if you can!
If not a journalist, what would you do? Have a regular sleeping pattern
Which person in the world would you most like to meet? Henry Cavill, but mostly just to make my friend Caulee jealous

MARK LANGDON'S WORLD OF MEAT

THE SALAMI TROPHY

When Ferenc Puskás was a young boy, he and his friends used to play football in a field in Kispest, on the outskirts of Budapest. One day, when he was eight, the local butcher, a man called Rudi, approached the boys. Puskás was worried. Was he there to complain about the window they had broken a few days earlier? Or about his cat, which they had kidnapped and sold to pay for tickets to watch Honvéd play? But no, he wanted them to put on a match for him, for which he offered a prize of some salami.

And so Puskás, in those days of hunger before the Second World War, learned that winning football matches was a good way to fill his belly. It was a lesson he never forgot: Billy Wright recalled watching in awe at the banquet after Hungary's 6–3 win over England at Wembley in 1953 as Puskás ate his way through an entire cheeseboard.

THE SALAMI SALESMAN AND THE TRIPEMEN

With two months of the 1933 Argentinian league season remaining, Gimnasia y Esgrima La Plata, almost unthinkably, led the table. Their unexpected upturn in form was, nobody doubted, down to their manager, a tall, angular, mysterious Hungarian called Imre Hirschl. He talked a good game, claimed to have played at a high level in Europe and had worked with the New York Hakoah team that had toured Argentina four years earlier, but nobody really had a clue who he was. All they knew was that he had dropped a lot of senior players, persuaded others to change position and then, after a rocky start (so rocky that his fellow Hungarian Béla Guttmann later claimed he had been trying to get sacked so he could use his pay-off to bring his wife and children to Argentina, only to stumble upon a successful formula, as though in a footballing version of *The Producers*), begun to win.

As it turned out, almost everything he said about his life in Europe was a lie. He had never played professionally, and his only involvement with Hakoah had been as a masseur. Before he left Budapest, Hirschl had in fact been a salesman for his uncles' salami business. Gimnasia was perhaps a natural home: they are nicknamed *los Triperos*, the Tripe Men, because so many of their fans worked in the meat-processing plants of nearby Berisso.

Hirschl and Gimnasia never won the league, undone by a mysterious string of controversial refereeing decisions in games against the traditional big five. But Hirschl moved on to River Plate, where in 1936 he won the double.

BANGERS AND CASH

When the West Germany midfielder Uli Hoeness was twenty-six and trying to get over the knee injury that would end his career, he was loaned from Bayern to FC Nürnberg. There, he had an idea. A few years earlier, he had been involved in talks between a butcher friend of his and Aldi about supplying Nürnberger sausages – they are small, almost like a chipolata – to the supermarket chain. Nothing had come of it because original Nürnbergers have to be made in Nuremberg. And now here he was in Nuremberg, where another friend of his, Werner Christoph Weiss, owned a small butchery. He got in touch with Aldi and, in 1985, after some trial and error with the recipe, HoWe sausages came into being. The company, now run by Hoeness's son Florian, has three hundred employees and produces around four million sausages a day.

It was while on a business trip to the US to sell sausages that Uli Hoeness, the long-time president of Bayern, arranged a secret rendezvous with Pep Guardiola and persuaded him to come to Munich as coach.

TURKEY, A MOCKING BIRD

As a young man, Jack Charlton was very easy to wind up – which, of course, only meant that his teammates wound him up whenever they got the chance. Because of his long neck, they called him 'Turkey', a nickname he hated. Matters came to a head at Christmas 1957, when Leeds United played away at Sunderland and stayed at the Seaburn Hotel on the seafront. Jack was also notoriously late, and so, knowing he would be last down to dinner the day before the game, the Leeds forward Bobby Forrest went into the kitchen, helped himself to a turkey's head and left it in Jack's place at the table. When Jack finally arrived, he erupted, grabbing a plate and hurling it against the wall of the restaurant. Sunderland won 2–1.

DISGRACE IN THE PORK MARKETS

For reasons nobody entirely understood, Johan Cruyff had always said he would retire at the age of thirty-one, so when his contract at Barcelona expired in the summer of 1978, his intention was to quit. He had enough money and he was exhausted. That was when a French friend called Michel Basilevitch, a former model who had begun to work as his agent, persuaded him to invest most of his fortune in a pig farm in Foradada, in the Spanish province of Lleida. A farm was built, with sties for three thousand pigs, but the holding company collapsed, with a loss of around £4 million in today's money. A penniless Cruyff was forced to accept a contract to play in the NASL with the LA Aztecs.

Cruyff being Cruyff, he later returned to Europe, won two league titles with Ajax and then, when they refused to offer him a new contract, won another with their great rivals Feyenoord, by which time he was thirty-seven.

THE LITTLE BIRD AND THE HOT-DOG MAN

In 2005, Ulf Lindberg, a hot-dog salesman from Halmstad, went to Brazil for the first time. Everywhere he went, he was surrounded by journalists, TV crews and photographers. He signed autographs, posed for photos and joined in a kickabout. It wasn't entirely unexpected, but for a very ordinary Swedish man, it was all extremely bizarre. Lindberg's life may have been unremarkable, but his father's had not been. His father was Garrincha, the Little Bird, perhaps the greatest winger in Brazil's history.

Garrincha had won the World Cup in Sweden in 1958, and the following year had returned on tour with his club, Botafogo. After an easy win in a friendly in Umeå in northern Sweden, most of the Botafogo players had stayed in the team's hotel, avoiding the cold. But Garrincha, typically, had gone out, met a woman and snuck into her bedroom while her parents watched TV downstairs.

The next day, the woman, her father and the police turned up at the hotel and demanded a blood sample. Nine months later, when she gave birth, Garrincha was back in Brazil, so the woman put her son up for adoption. In 1977, Garrincha casually mentioned in an interview that he had a son in Sweden whom he had never met. The newspapers went to work and found the boy, and for a time Ulf and his father corresponded. Halmstad, at the time managed by Roy Hodgson, offered Ulf a trial, but his rheumatism made a career in football impossible.

Six years later, Garrincha, suffering from the impact of his alcoholism, died, aged forty-nine. Ulf never met him.

JONATHAN WILSON

Full name: Jonathan Mark Wilson
Birthplace: Sunderland
Car: None
Previous/other clubs/media outlets: *FT, Independent, Sports Illustrated*
Job or trade before becoming a journalist: Dishwasher, bottle packer, data-entry clerk
Nickname: The Mackem-lele
Favourite player: Julio Arca
A player for the future: Pierre Ekwah
Favourite other podcast: *Football Clichés*
Childhood football hero: Shaun Elliott
Favourite other sport: Cricket
Other sportsperson you most admire: Ben Stokes
All-time favourite XI: Jim Montgomery; Darijo Srna, Hughie Wilson, Gary Bennett, Silvio Marzolini; Humberto Maschio, Franky Van der Elst, Luka Modrić; André Ayew, Niall Quinn, Allan Johnston
Most memorable match: Sunderland 2, Chelsea 1, FA Cup sixth-round replay, Roker Park, 1992
Biggest disappointment: Smacking a first-ball full toss straight to square leg in a game at the P. Sara Oval in Colombo
Best stadium visited: Roker Park
Favourite food and drink: Spaghetti alla puttanesca and Pinot Noir
Miscellaneous dislikes: Other people
Favourite music: Ennio Morricone
Favourite actor: David Suchet
Favourite actress: Joan Hickson
Favourite holiday destination: The Alps
Best film seen recently: *Paris, Texas*
Favourite TV show: *Endeavour*
Favourite activity on a day off: Cricket
Biggest influence on career: My mam
Superstitions: Never wear the no. 4 shirt
International honours: Have played cricket against both Iceland and the Vatican, and football for Tibet vs India
Personal ambition: To get a publisher to commission my book on Matthias Sindelar
If not a journalist, what would you do? Be a poor academic
Which person in the world would you most like to meet? Márton Bukovi

Full name: Robyn Elisabeth Cowen
Birthplace: Oxford
Car: Toyota Auris
Previous/other clubs/media outlets: BBC Radio Oxford
Job or trade before becoming a journalist: Law student
Nickname: Robynio
Favourite player: Vivianne Miedema
A player for the future: Gatlin O'Donkor
Favourite other podcast: *Top Flight Time Machine, Elis James and John Robins*
Childhood football hero: Alan Shearer

ROBYN COWEN

Favourite other sports: Tennis, karate
Other sportsperson you most admire: Serena Williams
Most memorable match: England 8, Norway 0, Women's Euros 2022, Brighton
Biggest disappointment: Being crap while commentating on my team in the FA Cup
Best stadium visited: As a fan, Stadio Olimpico; as a commentator, Brentford Community Stadium
Favourite food and drink: Most things on Footy Scran Twitter
Miscellaneous likes: Leisurewear, a good non-alcoholic beer, chocolate
Miscellaneous dislikes: Redacted (BBC employee…)
Favourite music: Anything on Heart '90s/'00s
Favourite actor: Michael Sheen
Favourite actress: Daisy May Cooper
Favourite holiday destination: Cornwall
Best film seen recently: *Bad Trip*
Favourite TV show: *Curb Your Enthusiasm*
Favourite activity on a day off: Film at home with friends and lots of calorific snacks
Biggest influence on career: BBC Radio Oxford sports editor Jerome Sale
Superstitions: None (after lots of therapy)
International honours: Welly-wanging champ, female division, Garsington village fete, 2006
Personal ambition: Not to get cancelled
If not a journalist, what would you do? As little as possible
Which person in the world would you most like to meet? Larry David

The FIFA of 'Tomorrow'

Gianni

FIFA Pictures presents a MOHAMMED BIN SALMAN production, a MOHAMMED BIN THANI film
GIANNI starring PATRICE MOTSEPE FATMA SAMOURA SALMAN BIN IBRAHIM AL KHALIFA LAMBERT MALTOCK
ALEJANDRO DOMÍNGUEZ VICTOR MONTAGLIANI VLADIMIR PUTIN as Putin SALT BAE as Himself and introducing GIANNI INFANTINO as Gianni
Executive Producer ZURICH ARRESTS Choreography by BRYAN SWANSON Music adapted by VÉRON MOSENGO-OMBA Production executive MATTHIAS GRAFSTRÖM
Supervising Editor DAVID FARRELLY Director of Photography GIANNI INFANTINO Music by HASSAN AL-THAWADI Lyrics by RICHARD CONWAY Screenplay by NASSER AL KHATER
Produced by MOHAMMED BIN SALMAN Directed by MOHAMMED BIN THANI

The stage play Gianni was originally presented at Champions League draws by Pedro Pinto Produced on the Nyon stage with Giorgio Marchetti Reshmin Chowdhury and Pavel Nedvěd's hair

FROM FIFA Book of the stage play by SEPP BLATTER Music of the stage play by JÉRÔME VALCKE Lyrics of the stage play by MICHEL PLATINI
AVAILABLE IN PAPERBACK FROM ALLTOTALLYFINE BOOKS ORIGINAL SOUNDTRACK ALBUM AVAILABLE ON ABOVEBOARD RECORDS AND TAPES

COMING THIS SUMMER

GET IT LAUNCHED!

Why must football deny itself so? At the game's heart lies a primal force too often ignored, a belief system written off as heretical by the passing-it-around, getting-it-on-the-deck orthodoxy. And yet, as any football match reaches those decisive moments when a single goal can alter the outcome, the cry will ring out, and without fail. 'Get it launched' is a release of pressure, an admission that the mixer is where true destiny lies.

And to suggest that such an approach is one-dimensional/reductive/reactionary is to fail to recognise the beauty of goals like the following, each of which shows off the variety of outcomes simply getting it launched might unlock.

THE BIG MAN: ERLING HAALAND
Manchester City vs Brighton, 2022

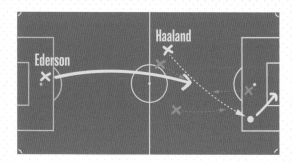

Pep Guardiola is a manager forever on a voyage of self-discovery, but the signing of Erling Haaland took the Catalan genius into a personal heart of darkness. Sure, he'd previously had Robert Lewandowski to call upon at Bayern Munich, but Haaland's size and speed added a cheat mode to sideline all that arty, fret-wankery, short-passing wibble. It also helped to have Ederson, a goalkeeper with the passing range of a 1970s schemer and distance judgement of Lee Trevino. Ping long, then smash past two defenders and a clearly frit Brighton goalie. Job done.

WHEN OPPORTUNITY KNOCKS: NIALL QUINN
Republic of Ireland vs Netherlands, 1990

Few players have met the definition of target man quite so readily as Niall Quinn, but in scoring his most famous goal, his was the role of poacher. Packie Bonner was the provider, almost knocking himself over with the momentum of his kick out of hand and into the Palermo night sky. Tony Cascarino and Berry van Aerle watched as the ball dropped like a stone, with the Dutch defender then slicing a panicked backpass that squirmed from keeper Hans van Breukelen's hands into the path of Quinn, who knocked in a goal that just about defined Jack Charlton's 'put 'em under pressure' philosophy.

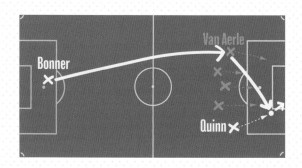

ADVENTURES IN SPACE: DENNIS BERGKAMP
Netherlands vs Argentina, 1998

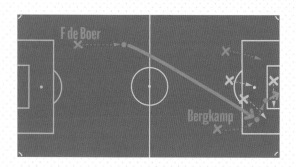

Dutch doctrines underpin what your average chalkboard, xG aficionado would recognise as modern football. The central, inescapable principle is that of creating and using space, and when deep into extra time Frank de Boer looked to go long, very long to Dennis Bergkamp as he meandered in the half-spaces, the defender was only following the lessons passed down by Rinus Michels, Johan Cruyff and Louis van Gaal, the game's Dutch masters. That few players can control the ball like a falling leaf and then bury it with such venom is the reason why such goals are so rarely scored, though quite often attempted.

GRACE UNDER PRESSURE: MICHAEL THOMAS
Arsenal vs Liverpool, 1989

The most decisive, thrilling goal of English football's prehistoric, ante-1992 period is a masterpiece of the genre. If the dying seconds are when a team in deficit is most likely to engage the launch pad, then here is a near-perfect execution. Michael Thomas's cool when everything was 'up for grabs now', in Brian Moore's quintessential description, is what the mind's eye recalls, but instead admire the quality of John Lukic releasing Lee Dixon, the right-back then lofting the ball exactly to where he expects Alan Smith to be. Smith deadens the ball and with one movement scoops through for Thomas to win the title for Arsenal.

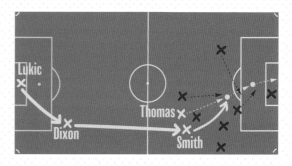

THE BEAUFORT SCALE: STEVE OGRIZOVIC
Coventry City vs Sheffield Wednesday, 1986

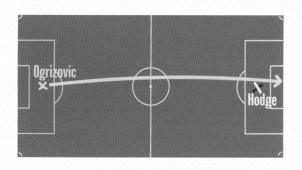

The late Gianluca Vialli shared a similar view to Jürgen Klopp: that frequent high winds in Britain have a profound impact on how the game is played. Away at Sheffield Wednesday, the Coventry perennial Steve Ogrizovic used his hammer of a right foot to engage a howling Hillsborough gale that was whipping off the Pennines to score the most direct open-play goal possible. His opposite number, Martin Hodge, stepped a yard forward, only for the ball's bounce to catch the breeze, loop over him and fade gently into the net. The rest of the match, a 2–2 draw, saw the unfortunate Hodge unable to kick past the halfway line, while Ogrizovic kept attempting to use the elements to repeat his trick.

HIT AND RUN: MAYNOR FIGUEROA
Wigan vs Stoke, 2009

Those who decry the launch-it philosophy condemn it as dull-witted. To do so ignores the free-form ingenuity it can encapsulate. Tony Pulis, a high priest of the long game, a pope of Position of Maximum Opportunity, found his Stoke team caught on the hop by the improvisational elan of the otherwise tough-tackling Honduran stopper Maynor Figueroa. Within a second of Rory Delap felling Scott Sinclair, from a couple of steps inside his own half Figueroa sent the free kick home. '[Thomas] Sørensen caught off his line,' said the BBC's Tony Gubba. In fact, the Stoke keeper was exactly where he was expected to be.

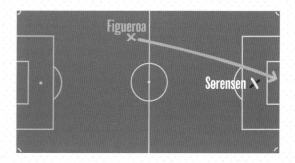

JOHN BREWIN

THE BEST OF
The Knowledge
with James Dart

THE WORST PENALTY SHOOT-OUT
What is the worst penalty shoot-out there has ever been?
(Mike Gibbons)

The 1986 European Cup final takes some beating. After Barcelona and Steaua Bucharest had played out 120 of the most tedious minutes of football ever witnessed in a major final, and with the score at 0–0, the game went to penalties. Both teams missed their first two, but the Romanians then found their shooting boots and knocked home their next two, with Barça twice more failing to beat Helmuth Duckadam in the Steaua goal. Having saved all four spot kicks from José Alexanko, Ángel Pedraza, Pichi Alonso and Marcos Alonso, enabling Steaua to run out 2–0 winners, Duckadam became known as 'The Hero of Seville'. Sadly, Duckadam, who at twenty-seven was reaching his peak years as a goalkeeper, was forced to retire shortly after his finest hour when an aneurysm was discovered in his right arm.

The 1973 Merdeka Tournament featured a pair of shoot-out stinkers: Thailand edged past Bangladesh 1–0 on penalties, while Singapore beat Cambodia by the same scoreline in another shoot-out. However, the world record is, quite predictably, held by a pair of English teams. In January 1998, the Under-10 sides Mickleover Lightning Blue Sox and Chellaston Boys faced off in the Derby Community Cup. The game finished 1–1, with the Blue Sox winning 2–1 on penalties, though not until a remarkable sixty-six spot kicks had been taken.

A FOOTBALL NIP/TUCK

Which players have gone under the cosmetic surgeon's knife to enhance their looks?
(Philip Genochio)

Rumours spread among the Brazilian press in 2009 that Ronaldo had undergone liposuction, but when asked directly whether he'd had the procedure, the forward replied cryptically: 'I don't know, I don't even know if I did. These are things we don't know . . . What I do with my private life is my business.'

There is no doubt about the former Colombia goalkeeper René Higuita, mind, who underwent surgery for all to see on the reality television show *Cambio Extremo* in 2005. 'I am tired of being ugly René, I want to be handsome René,' he declared. As reported in the *Observer*, 'Higuita had televised nose surgery, a silicone chin implant, skin peel, eyelid skin cut away, "aggressive" liposuction and abdominal muscle enhancement after being voted Colombia's "ugliest icon". After a month in isolation, Higuita revealed his brand-new look. "Bodily, I am perfect," he declared.'

Next up is Saša Ćurčić, once of Bolton, Aston Villa and Crystal Palace, whose wife Lisa told the *Sunday Mirror* in 1998 of the Serbian's nasal surgery. 'Some of [my friends] couldn't understand why I'd fallen for someone with such a big hooter,' she said. 'But I've never been attracted to pretty boys and I thought he had an interesting face and lovely eyes.' She went on to explain that Ćurčić was operated on at a private London hospital, having complained about problems with his breathing. 'Well, that was his story,' said Lisa. 'I think it was more to do with vanity because he was always telling me he'd like to have a nose like mine.'

Obviously, there is a swathe of players who have had operations that were necessitated by injuries received on the field of play. There are also off-field injuries which have required work. For instance, in 2010, Diego Maradona was bitten by his pet dog in Buenos Aires, which saw him head off to the local Los Arcos clinic for surgery on his upper lip.

Finally (and admittedly rather tenuously), plastic surgery can come back to haunt footballers, as it did with Lothar Matthäus. His estranged wife, Liliana, demanded that the former Germany captain foot the €2,800 bill for a breast augmentation reversal. 'I fail to see why I should pay for this and other plastic surgery bills,' Matthäus, who had paid for the initial augmentation as a school-leaving present, told *Bild*.

INJURED IN THEIR OWN TESTIMONIAL
Has there ever been a case of a professional footballer getting a serious injury during their testimonial?
(Andrew Wilson)

Ouch. These games are usually one rung down from friendlies on the ladder of intensity, so injuries are rare. But that wasn't the case in a pre-season testimonial for Denis Irwin at Old Trafford in August 2000, when Manchester United took on their neighbours City. Just four minutes into his big night, the stalwart was brought down in a tackle by the future president of Liberia, George Weah. As the *Guardian* reported, 'despite his gamest efforts, he limped reluctantly off'. After a standing ovation, Irwin 'looked none too pleased when Weah offered him an apologetic hand on the shoulder'. He was ruled out for a month.

Twenty years earlier, Johan Cruyff suffered severely wounded pride during his farewell at Ajax, when Bayern Munich left their goodwill at the airport and decided to run riot. They won 8–0.

WEIGHTY ISSUES
Has a player ever been given the boot by a club after his manager said he was too fat?
(Jim Cordes)

It's probably fortunate that William Foulkes strained into his shorts 120 years ago; can you imagine him turning up for pre-season these days, tipping the scales at 24 stones? Not that the goalkeeper himself cared, once saying: 'I don't mind what they call me, as long as they don't call me late for my lunch.' Nonetheless, Foulkes was never ditched for being too big-boned, unlike Neil Ruddock, who would eventually have weight clauses inserted in any contracts offered to him.

When Ruddock joined Crystal Palace in 2000, the club's chairman Simon Jordan recalled: 'Harry Redknapp told me to make sure I had a weight clause in his contract . . . 98 kilos, or whatever. And if he's over that, then fine him 10 per cent of his wages. That's the only way to ensure you get a fit and focused Ruddock.' Amid struggles to make the weight, the defender's contract was cancelled by mutual consent a year later, at which point he moved on to Swindon.

Things were no better at the County Ground, even after Ruddock lost a stone, and in August 2002, he was transfer-listed for being overweight (it was reported he could not fit into any of the eighty-six pairs of shorts owned by the club and had to have some custom-made). 'The manager, Andy King, has indicated that the player is not fit to play first-team football,' sniffed the chief executive, Mark Devlin. 'He is also unable to complete a full training regime alongside the other players.' Ruddock eventually left and went on to win £57,000 in unpaid wages at an employment tribunal.

In 2005, the Albion Rovers striker Mark Yardley left in acrimonious circumstances, claiming the club was attempting to ditch him after reports that he was troubling the scales. 'Yes, I am overweight, but I am not 20 stones, that's nonsense,' he said. 'I have not played a competitive game since last November, so I am obviously not match-fit. But I don't know where all this talk came from about my weight.'

Weighty issues transcend continents, and in 2008, the Vasco de Gama manager Renato Portaluppi had to battle bulging squad members. He eventually decided to fine players who were unable to shed their excess pounds. 'A footballer only learns in two ways: when he loses his place in the team or when he is fined,' declared Portaluppi, setting a $164 levy if anyone failed to shed the surplus inches around their midriff.

MOST OBSCURE SENDING-OFFS

Who's the person with the most obscure role to be sent off during a match, other than ballboys?
(Matthew Britton)

Mike Riley was having none of Kingsley Royal's antics during Reading's game against Newcastle in 2007, sending the giant lion mascot on his way for being too close to the pitch in his full replica kit. 'I can see where the referee was getting confused. He does look like so many of my players,' deadpanned manager Steve Coppell. At their next home match, Kingsley wore a T-shirt under his kit that proclaimed he was 'INNOCENT' and revealed it during a pretend goal celebration. A roar deal, all told.

There have been other incidents of misbehaving mascots falling foul of officialdom, with Bury's Robbie the Bobby – a policeman – managing to rack up three dismissals in as many months back in 2001: once for his part in a touchline brawl with Cardiff City counterpart Barclay the Bluebird, and twice for mooning supporters.

North of the border, the 2009 Battle of Douglas Park, a post-match tunnel brawl between the players and backroom teams of Hamilton and Hearts, resulted in the Jambos' masseur Alan Robson being shown the red card, along with three players. A few weeks earlier, Hamilton's elderly kitman, Danny Cunning, had earned himself a two-match ban after being sent to the stands for 'unacceptable conduct' early in the second half of a 2–2 draw between the Accies and Motherwell.

And finally, to the USA in 1981, where a PA announcer for the St Louis Steamers was dismissed at a Major Indoor Soccer League game after swinging a haymaker at a member of the visiting Buffalo Stallion. Kevin Slaten tried to punch Buffalo's John Dolinsky 'because the player, in a salty invective, called him the worst announcer in the league'.

THE FESTIVE AXE

Has a club ever been cruel enough to give their manager the boot on Christmas Day?
(Simon Briggs)

Heartless as it sounds, a club has been known to sack its manager on Jesus's birthday, and it was even brave enough to ruin the festivities for one José Mourinho. 'I was nine or ten years old, and my father [Félix] was sacked on Christmas Day,' recalled the Portuguese during an interview in 2004. 'He was a manager, the results had not been good. He lost a game on 22 or 23 December. On Christmas Day, the telephone rang and he was sacked in the middle of our lunch. So I know all about the ups and downs of football. I know that one day I will be sacked.' He wasn't wrong, aside from some of the story's details. His father was sacked by Rio Ave following a top-flight defeat to Covilhã in 1984, when Mourinho would have been twenty-one.

The Munich Anecdote

Stop Video

Mute

Share

Invite

Manage Participants

Chat

Nothing said during a live show has generated quite as much reaction as what has become known as 'The Munich Anecdote'. As Barry, improbably clad in a handmade orange silk shirt, completed his story and proudly lit up a fag, the other panellists struggled to cope with the horror of what they'd just heard.

For a little context, this was Barry's response to a question about what embarrassing incident from their pasts the panellists might use in a goal celebration . . .

00:59

I would return to my youth, when I was seventeen. I would travel to Munich with a throat infection while taking antibiotics. Then I would go on an all-night drinking session on strong Bavarian lager – against medical advice.

Then I would get on a packed U-Bahn in the morning rush hour while drunk. I would think I was about to unleash a little fart and then violently shit myself with a torrent of molten, hot, liquid defecation and clear the carriage at the next station. And then finish my celebration by trudging home to a campsite, with my jeans sodden, coloured brown, and all my mates laughing at me.

Ten years later, when I brought a nice English girl home to Birr to introduce her to my friends and family, the first thing one of them said to her, upon being introduced, was, 'Oh, hello. Has Barry told you about the time he shat himself in Munich?' To which she replied, 'No, he hasn't, but you can tell me all about it while he gets the drinks in.'

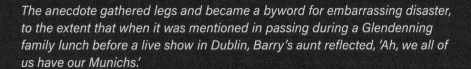

The anecdote gathered legs and became a byword for embarrassing disaster, to the extent that when it was mentioned in passing during a Glendenning family lunch before a live show in Dublin, Barry's aunt reflected, 'Ah, we all of us have our Munichs.'

This is a 'Munich' sent in by listener Stev that involves Barry, this time through no fault of his own, again making a spectacle of himself in Europe.

The year was 2015, the location was Amsterdam's regal Het Koninklijk Concertgebouw venue, where my partner and I had secured front-row tickets to see the Detroit techno wizard Jeff Mills perform a special concert with the North Netherlands Orchestra.

Having been a fan of Mills's lock grooves for over two decades, to experience such an occasion from such exceptional seats was something I was never likely to forget, but I thought a quick cheeky snap wouldn't go amiss, so drew out my iPhone and mid-track tried to capture a few photos. To avoid being the annoying twat who holds his phone aloft, I covertly tilted my phone upwards at chest level and used the side buttons to fire off a few frames, before calmly putting my phone back in my pocket, all while maintaining my gaze on the people making the parps and the clangs above.

Once the track finished and the applause had died down, Jeff stepped forward to a microphone and started to address the audience with a tale of yesteryear, but rather annoyingly someone could be heard quite brazenly holding up their end of a somewhat forthright conversation. I wasn't impressed and neither was Jeff, who glared down at the front rows and irritatingly referenced the rudeness of the person in question. 'Yeah, what a wanker,' I thought, but still the voice went on.

Now intrigued by what this musical heathen found more important than the performance before him, I listened more closely and realised I recognised the voice. It was Barry Glendenning, sourly debating the events of that week's Carabao Cup fixtures. It was then that I realised my attempt to blindly take photos of the gig had led me to inadvertently switch on the last thing I'd been listening to and push the volume up to max, and it was currently blaring out of my pocket – *Football Weekly*.

Slumping, embarrassed, into my seat, I fumbled around with the volume as the legend cut his tale short and went back to doing his thing. So, if you were in the audience that day, I would like to apologise for the angry Irishman bemoaning the Morecambe vs Bournemouth game. It wasn't his fault this time, it was mine.

Full name: Lars Elgheim Sivertsen
Birthplace: Stavanger, Norway
Car: None
Previous/other clubs/media outlets: *Josimar*, TV2, Betsson

LARS SIVERTSEN

Job or trade before becoming a journalist: Pizza maker/delivery driver, newspaper delivery driver, fruit-and-veg warehouse worker (I was a true artist with a pallet truck)
A player for the future: Erling Haaland's kids. Just getting that one in early
Favourite other podcast: *Second Captains*
Childhood football hero: Erik Thorstvedt
Favourite other sports: Floorball
All-time favourite XI: Heurelho Gomes; Timothée Atouba, Younes Kaboul, Paul Stalteri (Diesel is way too steady for this bunch, but every crime needs an innocent bystander); Stéphane Dalmat, Adel Taarabt, Tanguy Ndombele, Kevin-Prince Boateng, Érik Lamela; Frédéric Kanouté, Dimitar Berbatov (almost disqualified for also being actually brilliant). Some clubs have 'banter eras'; at Spurs it's just called 'the last thirty years'
Most memorable match: Ajax 2, Tottenham 3, Champions League semi-final second leg, 2019
Biggest disappointment: You'd think the final in Madrid would be the follow-up, but actually Norway at Euro 2000. I was thirteen and convinced we'd be good. We weren't
Best stadium visited: White Hart Lane (because I'm slow to get over things)
Favourite food and drink: Let's say Szechuan food with an appropriate wine pairing
Miscellaneous likes/dislikes: Filling out lists of favourite things because they all constantly change according to mood anyway
Favourite music: Kaizers Orchestra
Favourite actor: I don't know. Roy Keane?
Favourite holiday destination: Kerry in the summer with the girlfriend
Best film seen recently: *Everything Everywhere All at Once*
Favourite TV show: *The Wire* is the right answer, I guess, but I've also spent an unhealthy amount of time recently rewatching *The Thick of It* and *Veep*
International honours: I've played in the elite section of the Norwegian Brass Band Championships. That's . . . something?
Personal ambition: Stay employed for another year; have a fully functioning left leg again at some point

Full name: Troy Townsend
Birthplace: Hackney, London
Car: Public transport services
Previous/other clubs/media outlets: Redwood FC, Cheshunt, Slough Town, Boreham Wood, Leyton FC, Potters Bar, S&T Academy
Job or trade before becoming a journalist: Physical education tutor and owner of a business that used football to help disadvantaged kids
Nickname: Towno
A player for the future: Mateo Messi
Favourite other podcast: *The Conv3rsation* and *It Was All a Dream: The Football Academy Journey* (massive plug)
Childhood football hero: Pelé
Favourite other sports: Cricket and tennis
Other sportsperson you most admire: Muhammad Ali
All-time favourite XI: Pat Jennings; Chris Hughton, Franco Baresi, John Lacy, Roberto Carlos; Sammy McIlroy, Terry Yorath, Lionel Messi, Frank Worthington; Colin Lee, Ronaldo
Most memorable match: England 4, Montenegro 1, World Cup qualifier, October 2013 (Andros's first cap and first international goal)
Biggest disappointment: Failing to make the grade as a footballer
Best stadium visited: San Siro – but I wasn't allowed in
Favourite food and drink: Rice and peas with stew chicken
Miscellaneous likes: Things that make me smile
Miscellaneous dislikes: Fakeness
Favourite music: R&B, soul
Favourite actor: Denzel Washington
Favourite actress: Jennifer Aniston
Favourite holiday destination: Cyprus
Best film seen recently: *The Batman*
Favourite TV show: *24*, *Line of Duty*
Favourite activity on day off: What's a 'day off'?!
Biggest influence on career: Steve Browne, RIP, my business partner, who got me back into football and was a rock after the death of my son
Superstitions: I don't have any
International honours: Karaoke winner, Portugal, 2014
Personal ambition: To retire having made a difference
Which person in the world would you most like to meet? That would have been Muhammad Ali

TROY TOWNSEND

Ethan Pinnock
COMMEMORATIVE
NICKEL-BRASS BI-COLOUR £2 COIN

LIMITED
EDITION
original

Remember that back-post tap-in Ethan Pinnock scored for Brentford in their 3–3 draw against Liverpool on Saturday 25 September 2022? Hailed as an early contender for Goal of the Season by *Football Weekly*'s Barry Glendenning, it was outrageously omitted from the eventual shortlist – but the defender's first Premier League strike is being proudly commemorated with a new nickel–brass £2 coin.

By calling now on 0800–0800–PINNOCK you can own this special coin at the introductory price of £500. Only 5,999 of these new £2 coins are being produced, meaning that fewer than one in every 4,000 UK households can own one. Call now to ensure you don't miss out!

This coin benefits from the Shattons of London sell-out guarantee, which means any coins that are unsold on 31 December 2023 will be melted down and a personalised sell-out certificate issued, allowing you to be the owner of a potentially even rarer coin marking a special afternoon in the Jamaica international's career.

So to own this world-first Ethan Pinnock commemorative coin for just £500, call now! Purchases are limited to one per household, and yours is covered by a complete 60-day satisfaction guarantee and a 5-star Trust Pilot rating.

You Net!

CAN YOU IDENTIFY THE STADIUMS WHERE YOU'D HAVE FOUND THESE 1980S GOAL NETS?

1

2

3

4

5

6

2084

It was a bright, cold day in April, and the clocks were striking thirteen. Dave Fan, wearing the familiar red colours of Real Eurasia, head lowered against the vile wind, slipped quickly through the doors of Blatter Mansions, though not quickly enough to prevent a swirl of gritty dust from entering along with him.

The hallway smelled of boiled cabbage and old rag mats. At one end of it a coloured poster, too large for indoor display, had been tacked to the wall. It depicted simply an enormous face, more than a metre wide: the face of a man of about sixty-four, with a high hairline and a diffident air – Big BruVar, the leader of the regime. Dave, in his most private moments, admitted Big BruVar made him uneasy. But, of course, he would never say that, never even think it in public.

There was an hour till kick-off, plenty of time in which to order a grease-soaked pizza from OurPan's and have a little flutter with OurBet. This was the big one, the massive derby against Oceania United, their great rivals. Or at least that's what they said on OurSports 17, although Dave thought he remembered a time when the team they really hated was Sporting Eastasia. But where did that knowledge exist? Only in his own consciousness, which in any case must soon be annihilated. And if all others accepted the lie that OurSports imposed – if all records told the same tale – then the lie passed into history and became truth. 'Who controls the past,' ran the OurSports slogan, 'controls the future. Who controls the present controls the past.'

Dave thought he even remembered a past, long before the days when the first sixteen OurSports channels were devoted to implausibly violent cage fighting and children playing computer games, when there had been more than three clubs. He didn't believe what the weird old men said, that there had been a time when every community had a club and they were all part of a huge pyramid – he wasn't demented – but he thought maybe there had once been seven or eight teams, before the economics of state control drove the inflationary spiral that bankrupted the legacy clubs run by mere construction magnates and hedge funds. What romantic days those must have been, Dave mused, before checking himself. These were dangerous thoughts to be having.

Real Eurasia were at home, playing at OurStadium in Baku, one of their six officially sanctioned home grounds. They would be wearing red kit number four, one of six officially sanctioned home kits. Oceania United also wore red at home, as did Sporting Eastasia, so they would be wearing white away kit number six.

The enormous TV came on automatically as Dave entered the room. He caught the tail end of an advert. 'Baku! Bacchanals! Baked goods!' roared the voice of Drurybot IV, his favourite auto-commentator, trying to persuade him to order yet more OurGin and another box of OurPasties. Then it was time for the Five Minutes Hate. An image appeared on the screen of Gerry Frailman, a winger who had left Eurasia for Oceania a few months earlier. Dave heard a great swell of booing from the flats nearby and found the sound rolling from his own lips too. The image on the screen changed to show footage, slowed down to a thousandth of its original speed, of Frailman dribbling towards Gianluigi Brut. A challenge, and Frailman begins to fall. The footage stopped, went into reverse. Dave saw the challenge again, saw Frailman begin to go down. Rewind, forward. Rewind, forward. The bastard! The absolute bastard! He had been – there was no doubting it – *looking for contact*. He had *made the most of it*. That had cost them the Gianni Infantino Memorial Shield, that penalty. What an absolute shit! Dave found himself flicking V-signs at the TV, spitting and snarling. God, he hated Frailman.

Dave sat down again and considered the odds that flashed up on the screen. He registered a two OurUnit bet on eleven corners and put the same on Winston, the big Brazilian summer signing from Oceania, to score at any time. Another ad came on. There was Ernesto Mario Fisema, the recently retired Argentinian great, explaining how he owed his superior stamina to OurTabs, the athletes' vape. Another betting opportunity: Eurasia to win by two goals or more, he decided. Five OurUnits. That was half his daily pay gone on three bets, but so what? It mattered more when there was money on it.

And what did he work for, if not to have fun like this? The job – sending out endless pointless newsletters about the OurTen, the new short form of cricket between the two big London franchises that they were trying to promote – was miserable enough. Concentration of talent, that was what it was all about these days, that was what KPBot kept telling them. As if Dave had any idea what would attract the younger generation. Make it neon, make it noisy. That's what Mr Giles said. And never ask why the north had stopped producing fast bowlers.

Dave opened a can of OurAle as the game kicked off. That bastard Frailman got the ball. Judas! Brut slid in and sent him into the stand. Get in! Do him! A yellow card! What for? The game was paused so they could check it. Big BruVar's domed visage filled the screen. 'Checking . . . checking . . . checking . . . Buy OurGin, now! . . . Checking . . . checking . . . decision correct.' Christ. You couldn't touch anybody any more. A thin, querulous voice explained that the foul had not been dangerous enough to merit red but had been sufficiently forceful for the booking to stand. In the deepest recesses of his soul, Dave again thought bad things about BruVar.

Nothing happened in the first period. Secretly, Dave wondered whether the traditional format of twelve periods of five minutes each really was optimal, but that wasn't the sort of opinion you voiced these days. An ad for an OurCamp on the east coast caught his eye. That might be a fun break: a week of labour in the fruit fields, with as much OurAle and OurRoast as you wanted every night, maybe even some fun with OurGirls.

Nothing much happened in the second period either. Dave checked OurText. Everybody seemed to agree that James Milner was having an outstanding game for somebody of his age. So solid, so industrious. And there was a lot of chatter about the new pressing system that had been introduced by Eurasia's intense, shaven-headed coach, Theodor Habermas. During the quarter-time interval, a curly-haired young man in a tight black polo neck explained it using an electronic screen.

Dave didn't really understand but typed out his message on OurText anyway: 'Great packing of the half-spaces. Habermas = genius.' He opened a new message and typed: '@GerryFrailman Judas scum'. He went to close the app down but saw he had seven replies already: four called Habermas a fraud, two called him a nonce, and the other did both. Dave opened another can of OurAle.

It was still 0–0, with a minute of the twelfth period to go. It had been, Mottybot 7 said on commentary, an intriguing tactical contest, a game of cat and mouse. Dave reckoned that if he'd been brave enough to open up an illegal stream, JPbot 2 would have been far more scathing, in his lugubrious way. Maybe it was Lawrobot on co-comms with him: that would have been ideal for a game this dreary. Dave took a huge gulp of OurAle.

Suddenly, the defence opened up and Winston surged through. A chance? Not quite. The big Oceania centre-half forced him wide, where Frailman was tracking back. Penalty! Surely a penalty! Frailman had clipped his heel. Referee? Winston, pushing himself up from the grass, looked incredulous. Nothing. The referee slashed his hands through the air and play went on. Even Frailman, the Judas bastard, looked sheepish. A disgrace! A scandal! And in the derby . . . The ball went out for a throw-in in association with OurCheese. A BruVar check. Come on, come on. 'Checking . . . checking . . . checking . . . Buy OurGin, now! . . . Checking . . . checking . . . decision incorrect.' Penalty. 'The player,' the uncertain voice stuttered in explanation, 'has just knocked the forward. That's a foul.'

Dave gazed up at the enormous face of Big BruVar. Forty years it had taken him to learn what kind of smile was hidden beneath the wide forehead. O cruel, needless misunderstanding! O stubborn, self-willed exile from the loving breast! Two booze-scented tears trickled down the sides of his nose. But it was all right, everything was all right, the struggle was finished. He had won the victory over himself. He loved Peter Walton.

Jonathan Wilson

Focus on SUZY WRACK

Full name: Suzanne Linda Beishon Wrack

Birthplace: Hackney

Car: Ford Focus

Previous/other clubs/media outlets: BBC Sport, *Sunday Times*, Reach plc, *Morning Star*

Job or trade before becoming a journalist: I studied architecture at university, then worked in design and comms for a bit

Nickname: Suzy, Wrack the Hack (thanks, Jo Currie), Studio Rat (thanks, automatic transcription software)

A player for the future: Jess Park

Favourite other podcast: *My Therapist Ghosted Me*

Childhood football hero: Dennis Bergkamp

Favourite other sports: There's other sports?! Tennis

Other sportsperson you most admire: Serena Williams

All-time favourite XI: Mary Earps; Lucy Bronze, Leah Williamson, Tony Adams, Héctor Bellerín; Jill Scott, Megan Rapinoe; Jake Daniels, Vivianne Miedema, Marcus Rashford; Ian Wright

Most memorable match: The Lionesses winning Euro 2022 at Wembley against Germany

Biggest disappointment: Arsenal's 1999 FA Cup semi-final defeat

Best stadium visited: The Dripping Pan

Favourite food and drink: A proper Italian pizza and a fruity cider

Miscellaneous likes: Art, architecture, macaroni cheese, playing guitar

Miscellaneous dislikes: People who walk down the street expecting everyone else (me) to move out of their way, seafood, Tottenham

Favourite music: Pretty eclectic, but folk

Favourite actor: Steve Buscemi

Favourite actress: Olivia Colman

Favourite holiday destination: Iceland

Best film seen recently: *The Banshees of Inisherin*

Favourite TV show: *The Wire*

Favourite activity on day off: Drawing, lino-cutting – something arty

Biggest influence on career: Vikki Orvice, Anna Kessel, all the Women in Football bunch

Superstitions: I didn't wear Arsenal stuff on match days, until I left a ring on by mistake on the day Arsenal Women beat the European champions Lyon 5–0. Now I can't take it off. Ever

International honours: Well, I own about twenty baseball caps – does that count? Otherwise, my AIPS award for best colour piece on the investigation into the abuses suffered by the Afghanistan women's national team is about as close as I get

Personal ambition: To see women's football journalism valued as much as men's, and to finish learning the guitar

If not a journalist, what would you do? Architect or graphic designer

Which person in the world would you most like to meet? Taylor Swift should be my friend

Focus on ELIS JAMES

Full name: Owain Elis James

Birthplace: Haverfordwest, Wales

Car: 2010 Volkswagen Golf

Job or trade before becoming a journalist: Competent stand-up comedian

Nickname: Elis-D, Furby, El, El-Plate

A player for the future: Oli Cooper, and if a time machine is invented, Ivor Allchurch

Favourite other podcast: *Three Bean Salad*

Childhood football hero: Ian Rush

Favourite other sports: Boxing

Other sportsperson you most admire: Gareth Bale, Max Rushden

All-time favourite XI: Neville Southall; Chris Gunter, Kevin Ratcliffe, Franco Baresi, Ben Davies; Joe Allen, Andrea Pirlo, Aaron Ramsey; Cliff Jones, Jimmy Greaves, Gareth Bale

Most memorable match: Wales 3, Russia 0, Euro 2016

Biggest disappointment: Wales 1, Romania 2, National Stadium, Cardiff, 17 November 1993

Best stadium visited: The Vetch Field, Swansea

Favourite food and drink: Lasagne, the kind of pretentious coffee idiots like, squash

Favourite music: Gorky's Zygotic Mynci, Pavement, theme tunes to *Auf Wiedersehen*, *Pet* and *Minder*

Favourite actor: Robert De Niro

Favourite actress: Jennifer Saunders

Favourite holiday destination: Spain, Pembrokeshire

Best film seen recently: Wallace and Gromit in *The Wrong Trousers*

Favourite TV show: *Football Focus*

Favourite activity on day off: Gentle cycle to warm down, going on my phone as my kids are at soft play

Biggest influence on career: Barney Ronay, Steve Coogan, Hugh McIlvanney

Superstitions: I have lucky pants, shirt, watch and coat for Wales and Swansea games, the powers of which seem to be waning badly

International honours: BBC Radio 5 Live *Fighting Talk*'s Rookie of the Year 2015–16, BBC Radio 5 Live's Fighting Talk Champion of Champions 2019–20, So You Think You're Funny New Act of the Year semi-finalist, 2007

Personal ambition: To work out which formation a team is playing in without having to read it in the match report of a trusted journalist

If not a journalist, what would you do? Referring to myself as a journalist is a bit much, but if comedy, podcasting and the radio went wrong, I would like to be a cycle courier or work in a shop

Which person in the world would you most like to meet? Aaron Ramsey, Paul McCartney

~~Humble~~ *Beginnings*

CB1 was a tough place to grow up. The harp in the music room wasn't even full size. And it was wildly out of tune. The piano was only an upright. My mountain bike had just two cogs at the front. Our school didn't have its own swimming pool. If I was going to make something of myself, it was going to be the hard way . . .

Stealing the League Cup

My summer job was as a punt chauffeur on the River Cam. I wore a boater and waistcoat, which was probably the uniform rather than a personal choice. Towards the end of summer 2001, ITV Digital bought the rights to the League Cup. The first game they showed was Cambridge United vs West Brom. Someone worked out later that the audience was so small that rather than showing it on TV, it would have been cheaper to pay for all the viewers to go to the game, including travel.

Before the game, they were filming some pre-match stuff. As I punted a group of twelve down the river, I saw the League Cup being pushed towards me on an empty boat. As it sidled past, I leaned down, picked it up and carried on my way. It's heavier than you expect. A lot of producers with earpieces shat themselves and started chasing me. I gave the cup back.

A Question for Jodie Marsh

In the summer of 2008, I started doing the late show on talkSPORT. Back then, it was three hours of current affairs. I was doing the show because they had sacked James Whale. I'd get nice texts from listeners, asking, 'Where's James, you parasite?' Eric in Belfast texted to say, 'I don't know who you are mate but you've got the personality of a breeze block.' That led to a two-hour phone-in on the worst inanimate object to be compared to. A lesson learned: never waste material.

One morning, the producer rang. We talked through the issues, and just before hanging up, she said, 'Oh, by the way, Jodie Marsh will be with you from 11 p.m. until 1 a.m.'

'OK,' I said. I didn't know Jodie Marsh, but it's always good to co-present with someone new (unless perhaps they're a cyclist and knight of the realm, but that's another story).

We did the first hour all fine – a phone-in on how long terror suspects should be imprisoned without charge and something about plastic bags. Jodie arrived. I wasn't quite sure what she usually did, but she said she'd answer anything the listeners wanted to ask, which given she was a glamour model who'd just done *Celebrity Big Brother* seemed a little risky, but what else were we going to do?

We opened the phone lines. Dave in Clacton called.

'Hi, Dave.'

'Hello, Max.'

'You have a question for Jodie.'

'Yeah, I do. She's happy to answer anything, right?'

With a certain anxiety: 'Jodie, you're happy to answer anything?'

'Sure.'

With a mounting sense of dread: 'Great. Dave, away you go.'

'Jodie, I'm blind and on dialysis. How do I get a mortgage?'

Silence.

The Big Break

I was hosting the BBC London 94.9 breakfast show. It had been an incredible success – the highlight of which was noticing one day that unleaded petrol was on sale at 94.9 pence a litre, the best possible viral marketing campaign. Although I've moved past repeating jokes now, at the time I loved to hammer them into the ground. So all I talked about for weeks was petrol costing 94.9p. The boss loved it, but also removed me from the show at the first opportunity. You don't want to unbalance a team by standing out from your peers and colleagues – another valuable lesson learned.

I filmed a showreel round the back of the office. In it I wandered about looking at things, before the grand finale: me sitting on a sofa next to Vanessa Feltz, saying, 'TV shows are normally people on sofas chatting to famous people, thank you for your time, goodbye.' Then Vanessa said goodbye. The reel was a huge success. I sent it off to the BBC, ITV, Channel 4, Sky – every channel possible in the UK. They all ignored it. Except for the Travel Channel, who said I was boring – 'not edgy enough' was the exact quote.

Eventually, Sky rang me up, and we talked about Dion Dublin for an hour. A month later, they gave me a two-year deal to host *Soccer AM*. No screen test. No audition. No pilot. Nothing. So I did that for seven years.

I had an audition for *Blue Peter* on the same day as getting *Soccer AM*. I had to learn the history of Lego and spray someone with a water pistol. I was offered that job, too. Weird day.

The Record Contract

I would often mention my clarinet on *Soccer AM*. The producer didn't like it. 'Northerners will think you're gay,' he said, affectionately. Anyway, I played the *EastEnders* theme on it while Dion Dublin played the Dube. What a moment.

The singer Amy Macdonald came on the show, and I explained that her album was lacking some jazz clarinet. So she suggested I played on her next single. She actually meant it. So I popped along to a studio and recorded the part, filmed the video – playing a busker in some excellent boot-cut jeans – and played in an encore at the Hammersmith Apollo in front of 5,000 people.

While we were in the studio, I started humming along to a song. 'You can sing,' said Amy's manager. 'Why don't I sign you?' We went for a coffee, and he rang Warner Music, and they gave me thousands of pounds to write an album. I didn't write an album.

The Microwave

Christmas Day 2012. I was hosting. Aunty Gay had brought a microwaveable Christmas pudding. I didn't have a microwave. My neighbour was superstar DJ Trevor Nelson. He'd occasionally come over to watch *Super Sunday*. Or we'd have a round of golf. Lovely chap. He owned more vinyl than me. And his flat was bigger. I called him to see if he had a microwave. He had a spare one. I borrowed it. And didn't give it back for eleven years. He got a lot of mileage out of the story, eventually moving to Barnet with all his extra money. The microwave exploded in the spring of 2022.

I Met My Wife on a Volcano

I met my wife on a volcano. We are very happy.

Mick Hucknall and Pelé

Richard Keys was on stage. 'And as everyone knows,' he said, 'one of Pelé's greatest friends is Mick Hucknall.'

The room nodded in agreement. I was confused. I didn't know. Of course both Pelé and Mick Hucknall needed friends. We all do. And perhaps there's no reason why Mick Hucknall and Pelé shouldn't have been friends. But Mick Hucknall and Pelé wasn't a relationship I had pencilled in.

'And as everyone knows,' Keys went on, 'Pelé is the godfather to one of Mick Hucknall's children.' It might have been the other way round. I forget. The room again nodded along. I looked around to see if anyone thought this was as batshit as I did. Nope.

'And, of course, Mick wouldn't miss this evening for the world.' As he finished those words, a backing track of 'Stars' blared out of the speakers.

Mick arrived on stage with white trousers on and sang 'Stars' to Pelé. This was an unexpected serenading.

Between me and Mick and Pelé sat Roy Hodgson and Ray Lewington, mouthing the lyrics.

Subaru

I had my Subaru XV stolen in Northcote, Melbourne, in late January 2023. Registration APS514. Did you take it? Some weeks later, the police called. I got it back, and it was unharmed.

JOHN BREWIN'S
▼ POP PICKS ▶

[ADOPTS RADIO 1 DJ'S VOICE.] **HEY THERE, POP PICKERS. CUE THE MUSIC.**
[PHIL LYNOTT'S 'YELLOW PEARL' BLARES IN THE BACKGROUND.]

Once upon a time, football and the pop charts rarely met. Sure, maybe Paul McCartney attended the 1968 FA Cup final – Jeff Astle's winning goal and all that – despite long hiding his Evertonian leanings. And Phil Spector cut together some John Lennon rantings, including Matt Busby's name, amid the free-form jam that made up 'Dig It' on *Let It Be*, the Beatles' last album.

'Get Back'? Not arf, mate.

But before that, the most exposure to football those four lovable moptops from Liverpool got was in their Hamburg days, when the Fabs did their best to avoid drunken British servicemen. 'After a few drinks, they'd start shouting "Up Liverpool" or "Up Pompey"', said John. Risky business? You betcha.

Despite Rod the Mod ballooning balls into the crowd, Elton owning Watford and Geezer Butler from Black Sabbath's ever-present Aston Villa scarf, it wasn't until the 1990s that football and pop music properly entwined, as those Gallagher boys married them in true bovine style. Britpop, you say? Suddenly, every haircut indie-landfill band were wearing football shirts on Saturday mornings, during *Soccer AM*'s Andy Goldstein glory days.

But that all ignored a proud tradition of footballers, back in the days when they weren't on £300,000 a week, looking to make a fast buck by releasing a pop single. Almost without exception, they showed it really wasn't as easy as it looked. Turkeys are not just for Christmas, mate. All right!

Look out on social media for the Spotify playlist (just don't mention it to Philippe). And here's our chart top-ten rundown. Who will be the week's toppermost of the poppermost? All right?

Not arf!

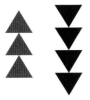

10. RUUD GULLIT, 'FREE ME' (1984)

He brought sexy football to the fashionable King's Road and had a fall-out with Alan Shearer, but Ruud was known as a footballer with a social conscience. Unmistakably inspired by Bob Marley, though with a tinge of UB40's pop-reggae stylings, he wasn't too bad on lead vocals. The title 'Free Me' referred to South African apartheid rather than a contract dispute with Feyenoord.

9. BOLI & WADDLE, 'WE'VE GOT A FEELING' (1991)

It may come as a surprise to those who check his Twitter these days, but Chris Waddle was once a continental prince. Singing partner Basile Boli, meanwhile, was the only man mad/brave enough to stick the nut on Stuart 'Psycho' Pearce. Together, they conjured up an African-influenced floor-filler you might have heard while sipping Taboo and Mirage down your average Euro meat market. Listen carefully for Waddler's Arthur Bostrom-inspired rhyming.

8. TERRY VENABLES, 'WHAT DO YOU WANT TO MAKE THOSE EYES AT ME FOR?' (1974)

Long before he was El Tel of Barcelona, Venables had his eyes on wider stardom than merely being QPR's deep-lying schemer. To go with penning private-detective novels and a TV series, which would later inspire Steve Bruce's literary career, he fancied himself as the Tony Bennett of soccer. Here, Tel takes on a Broadway standard that none other than Shakin' Stevens would do a far better job of.

7. ANDREW COLE, 'OUTSTANDING' (1999)

While he and Dwight Yorke were pairing up to score together – both on and off the pitch – during Manchester United's Treble season, Coley attempted to crash the charts. A cover of the Gap Band classic, Cole added his own rhymes in a way that wasn't always convincing.

6. PELÉ AND SÉRGIO MENDES, 'MEU MUNDO É UMA BOLA' (1977)

His playing days were coming to an end, and Viagra was just a glint in a pharmacist's eye, so the great man launched a pop career. Using Brazil's bossa nova/funk overlord Mendes as his accompaniment was cheating, but a pleasant enough cocktail-bar ditty resulted. 'My World Is a Ball' is the English translation, pun presumably intended.

5. PAUL GASCOIGNE, 'GEORDIE BOYS' (1990)

The difficult follow-up to 'Fog on the Tyne'. Abandoning the lyrics of Lindisfarne's Alan Hull, Gazza tried to ride the crest of the inflatable-breasts wave that followed Italia '90 with toy-town techno. He raps rather woodenly, celebrating Newcastle Brown Ale and those who drink it, referencing what Graham Taylor would soon refer to as 'refuelling'. This proved to be Gazza's last single, reaching number 31 – still four higher than The Fall ever managed.

4. JOHAN CRUYFF, 'OEI OEI OEI' (1969)

Released before he hit true worldwide fame, though Cruyff had already developed a taste for spin-off lucre. He always was ahead of the game. A brass-heavy piece of the type of schlager that makes zero sense across the North Sea ensued.

3. IAN WRIGHT, 'DO THE RIGHT THING' (1993)

These days a national treasure, Wrighty doesn't always wish to be reminded of his younger self. Perhaps the former presenter of *Friday Night's All Wright* might be kinder to the single he wrote and performed with Chris Lowe of the Pet Shop Boys. Atop a Masters at Work-style garage backing, Wrighty shows he can actually sing, and Haçienda regulars would have been none the wiser that they were grooving to the tones of Arsenal's star striker.

2. KEVIN KEEGAN, 'HEAD OVER HEELS IN LOVE' (1979)

The man who made the name Kevin and bubble perms popular in Germany was never shy of a commercial cash-in. Using the jaunty template of co-writer Pete Spencer's former band Smokie – of 'Living Next Door to Alice' fame – Henry Cooper's former partner in Brut-splashing and manly shower chat kept it simple, cheesy and hooky.

1. GLENN & CHRIS, 'DIAMOND LIGHTS' (1987)

A second top-ten appearance for Chris Waddle, but it's singing partner Glenn Hoddle who takes centre-stage in this all-time classic. Powered by a mid-1980s electronic emulator backbeat, it veers close to *101*-era Depeche Mode, minus the bondage gear. Glenn's falsetto as they hit the chorus conjures up that time Mark Falco got creative with the Deep Heat, while Waddler's Ian Curtis-esque drone holds down the low end.

Producer Joel's CASEBOOK

Joel Grove is the producer of *Football Weekly*. Find out whether you could do his job by taking this aptitude test.

Scenario 1

Jordan Jarrett-Bryan has just appeared on the show and during the recording delivered a take so hot (e.g. Son Heung-min is a bastard or Kevin De Bruyne has no left foot) that you know it'll set the internet ablaze and have commenters below the line calling for blood.

Do you:

a) Cut the section in question and fill the gap with the oddly soothing sound of Barry smoking?

b) Don't edit a thing and run the take? The hits and listens are worth more than Jordan's sanity; indeed, he's so used to fire-fighting after each appearance that he's vying for a part in the sequel to *Backdraft*.

c) Send the clip to Liam McClair to be transformed into weirdly hypnotic music?

d) Ignore the issue and assume Max can deal with it?

Scenario 2

It's 11 p.m., the night before an 8 a.m. recording, and Philippe Auclair is on the panel. He sends you a scanned PDF via WhatsApp detailing a scandal involving Gianni Infantino, FIFA and the Bolivian FA. Despite some heavy googling, you can find no other evidence of this story online.

Do you:

a) Set your alarm for 6 a.m. and put the *Guardian* lawyers on high alert? There's no way you can stop Philippe from sharing this story, and you agree it's probably more important than the stuff you have in the running order about Dagenham & Redbridge's new mascot. However, you'll need to warn Philippe that his ten-minute detailed retelling of the story will probably be cut down to a nice thirty-second sizzle reel of the best bits.

b) Insist the Dagenham & Redbridge mascot story is too big to cut – no room for Bolivia?

c) Ring Gianni's PR hotline and get a FIFA hit squad to deal with Philippe?

d) Ignore the issue and just press 'mute' when Philippe is speaking?

Scenario 3

You've finished recording the podcast. Five minutes after waving everyone goodbye on the Zoom call, it's announced that Frank Lampard/David Moyes/Graham Potter/Dean Smith has been sacked, rendering a good ten minutes of the show useless.

Do you:

a) Ignore it till next time? It's only Everton/West Ham/Chelsea/Aston Villa.

b) Get everybody back together and re-record the whole show, insisting that when the studio in Glasgow forgot to record the podcast that one time, the second take was better?

c) Call Max, ask him to record a voice note and run it at the top of the show? Remember: despite wrapping only five minutes earlier, Max will somehow be twenty miles and two hours away from his recording equipment. Or asleep.

d) Quit on the spot and focus on your other podcast about whichever lower-league side you support?

Scenario 4

You are due on stage at the Hackney Empire in five minutes, and Barry has finally had an idea for the running order. It involves a video clip he cannot find, nor can he really remember any of its details, but he is certain he wants it to be shown in the first ten minutes.

Do you:

a) Write 'STALL FOR TIME' in the script you share with Max as you desperately search Twitter, your hard drive and all three of the personal WhatsApps Barry has sent you in your three years working at the *Guardian*, eventually finding the video approximately ten seconds before Baz cues it up to be seen by an audience of 1,200?

b) Tell him it's not possible and hope the flow of booze means he'll have forgotten all about it by the end of the show?

c) Lock the doors, delay the start and refuse anybody admission until you finally track the video down?

d) Refuse to pay any of the participants and use the proceeds of the show to treat your girlfriend to a trip around Europe?

Scenario 5

Sid Lowe has not replied to any of your last six WhatsApp messages. You are quickly running out of ways of rewording the phrase 'Do you fancy doing ten minutes on *Football Weekly* this Tuesday to talk about La Liga?' But this Tuesday you desperately need him: it's been *El Clásico*, and Real Sociedad have signed Ross Barkley.

Do you:

a) Ignore it? Jesus, who cares about La Liga these days . . .

b) Send Sid another WhatsApp, while covering the rest of your screen with your hand so as not to remind yourself of previous attempts? Failing that, with your tail between your legs, ask Max to ask him? Sid *always* replies to the talent.

c) Ask Lars if he's got any views? (He will have.)

d) Join a conspiracy with several other *Football Weekly* regulars to split from the show? After all, it's always been your dream to voice ads for some device to shave your nether regions.

Joel's answers: 1a; 2b; 3c; 4a; 5b

BEDNAREK OR VESTERGAARD?

IN 2017, the Polish centre-back Jan Bednarek joined Southampton from Lech Poznań. A year later, the Danish centre-back Jannik Vestergaard joined Southampton from Borussia Mönchengladbach. Since when, despite them having completely different names and looking nothing like each other, nobody involved with *Football Weekly* has been capable of telling them apart.

But let's find out if you can tell your Jan from your Jannik by playing Bednarek or Vestergaard? Below is a list of ten facts. All you have to do is decide of which centre-back each is true.

1. I scored a comical own goal against Wolves in Nathan Jones's last game as Southampton manager. *Am I Bednarek or Vestergaard?*

2. I began my career with Hoffenheim. *Am I Bednarek or Vestergaard?*

3. I made my debut for Southampton in a 2–0 win over Wolves in the League Cup. *Am I Bednarek or Vestergaard?*

4. I left Southampton to join Leicester City. *Am I Bednarek or Vestergaard?*

5. My brother Filip is a professional goalkeeper. *Am I Bednarek or Vestergaard?*

6. I scored my first goal for my country in a 1–0 win over Japan at the 2018 World Cup. *Am I Bednarek or Vestergaard?*

7. My grandfather Hannes Schröers and uncle Jan Schröers both played for Fortuna Düsseldorf. *Am I Bednarek or Vestergaard?*

8. I scored in a 2–1 win over the Czech Republic in the opening game of the 2015 Under-21 European Championship. *Am I Bednarek or Vestergaard?*

9. I have a dog called Brady. *Am I Bednarek or Vestergaard?*

10. I left Southampton to join Aston Villa on loan, before being recalled. *Am I Bednarek or Vestergaard?*

ANSWERS

1. B, 2. V, 3. B, 4. V, 5. B, 6. B, 7. V, 8. B, 9. V, 10. B

INCIDENTAL FOOTBALL

IN MODERN LIFE, FOOTBALL IS ALMOST EVER-PRESENT, the constant backdrop, always there on screens and in conversations, which presents a problem for scriptwriters and directors. To ignore it is unrealistic, but to include it without due care and attention is to risk demolishing credibility or undermining carefully established timelines. We present six examples of football references in mainstream drama.

TINKER TAILOR SOLDIER SPY (1979)

On the night of Operation Testify, when Jim Prideaux is betrayed in Brno, we see Sam Collins, the duty officer at the Circus, having a couple of cans of beer while watching a match on a black-and-white portable. The commentator is clearly Barry Davies, and he mentions Paul Mariner, Clive Woods, Arnold Mühren and John Wark, so we know this is Ipswich Town. Davies commentated on three Ipswich games for *Match of the Day* between Mühren joining in 1978 and 1979, when *Tinker Tailor Soldier Spy* aired. But Ipswich are wearing white, which means this is almost certainly an away game against a team who wore blue. In two of Davies's three games, Ipswich played teams who wore red, leaving Manchester City against Ipswich in November 1978 as the sole possibility.

There is corroboratory evidence. Davies talks of defensive weaknesses having cost Ipswich's opponents the match – and Ipswich did in fact beat City 2–1. Pausing the programme as Mariner receives treatment shows the non-Ipswich number 5 walking away with his back to the camera. It's a stretch to say he could categorically be identified as Dave Watson, but he is the right height and build, with the right hair, and, crucially, he is wearing the captain's armband – as Watson did that day.

In the television series, then, it can be said with some certainty that Testify took place as Kazimierz Deyna made his City debut on the night of 25 November 1978, and going by the start time and length of the highlights, duty officer Collins is drinking his beer shortly after 10.30 p.m. The novel, though, was published in 1974. In it, Collins confirms Testify took place on a Saturday – which, as the previous Thursday is given as 19 October, must have been the 21st. 21 October was a Saturday in 1972, which means that had the adaptation wished to be absolutely faithful to the book – maintaining the same time frame and year (although *Match of the Day* started five minutes earlier in 1972) – Collins should really have been watching Davies commentate on Leeds 1, Coventry 1.

The
English
Patient

(1996)

When Hardy is killed while celebrating the end of the Second World War, Kip and Hana find a red-and-white-striped football scarf bearing a Sunderland badge among his few effects. This is problematic for a number of reasons. Although scarves in club colours became popular from the 1920s onwards, and so it's plausible a bomb-disposal expert in 1945 would have one, they were usually hand-knitted and would usually not have featured club crests – and certainly not a club crest that wasn't introduced until 1976. The scarf was apparently a joke played by the crew at the expense of the actor who played Hardy, the Newcastle-supporting Kevin Whateley (although I'm almost certain Whateley sat behind me at a pre-season friendly between Sligo Rovers and Sunderland in 1996).

There is a curious foreshadowing of this in *Auf Wiedersehen, Pet* (1983). In the second episode of the first season, Whateley's character, Neville, finds an unexploded bomb while kicking a football about and becomes a hero on the site. In the following episode, he is unable to join Dennis and Oz as they travel to Liège to watch Sunderland play a friendly.

HANNIBAL (2001)

In *Hannibal*, the sequel to *The Silence of the Lambs*, as FBI agent Clarice Starling chases up Italian investigators about a missing tape, a television in the background at the police station is showing a football match. The clip is six seconds long, and for half of that all that can be seen is the top of a player's head and the pitch behind him. But as the camera pans back, the player is easily identifiable as Julian Joachim, wearing a claret-and-pale-blue-striped Aston Villa shirt. Right at the end of the clip, the coverage cuts to show a goal frame. The match is clearly at Wembley, and so the game can be identified as the 2000 FA Cup final, in which Villa lost 0–1 to Chelsea.

As Joachim came on as a 79th-minute substitute and the game kicked off at 3 p.m., we can say, assuming this is a live broadcast, that the scene is taking place between 4.34 p.m. and 4.45 p.m. on 20 May 2000. The Italian domestic season had come to an end two days earlier, Sven-Göran Eriksson's Lazio drawing 0–0 away to Inter to win the Coppa Italia 2–1 on aggregate.

THE DAY AFTER TOMORROW
(2004)

A scientist at a remote weather station in Scotland is watching a Champions League match on television. 'Welcome back to Glasgow, Scotland, where Manchester United leads 3–1 over home-town Celtic,' a presenter with a Scottish accent says, before handing over to the commentator, a Donald McFarland. Alarm bells, obviously, are ringing already. 'Home-town Celtic?' Who would say that? And where have the viewers been to be welcomed back? It's not the start of the second half – indeed, it's stipulated the game is 63 minutes in. It's not, for instance, a 1980s Test match that you might cut away from for a horse race or the news.

But it gets worse. United can be readily identified: Ryan Giggs strides through the midfield and Ruud van Nistelrooy scores, but the other team is not in green-and-white hoops but in dark blue with a yellow band across the chest. It's the happily distinctive kit of Boca Juniors, and it doesn't take much to work out that this is actually a pre-season friendly at Old Trafford in 2002, in which United beat Boca 2–0.

LOST
(2007)

In a flashback, Desmond tries to explain to Ruth (and her ludicrous Scottish accent) that he walked out on her a week before their wedding because he had a 'calling'; scared of where his life was going, he'd got drunk, passed out and come around, to find the brother of a religious order offering him help. She sneers and says that in their six years together, the closest he had come to 'a religious experience' was 'Celtic winning the Cup'. That seems weirdly generic for a team as successful as Celtic; the only time when it would be at all clear which Cup she was referring to is during the period between 20 May 1989 and 30 November 1997, when Celtic won only one trophy – the Scottish Cup in 1995. It seems safe to assume, then, that the reference is to their victory over Airdrieonians in that final, Pierre van Hooijdonk heading in Tosh McKinlay's cross after nine minutes for the only goal of the game.

ENDEAVOUR
(2020)

The prequel to *Inspector Morse* has expended an astonishing amount of effort in recreating the 1960s, from clothing to cars to attitudes. Its attitude to football, though, is weirdly, perhaps unforgivably, lax. An episode first screened in February 2020 shows Inspector Thursday watching the football scores on television in January 1970. Shockingly, they are not even listed in alphabetical order. That the initial letters of the first five home sides spell out 'COLIN' – a nod to Colin Dexter, who wrote the *Morse* novels and had a cameo in each episode of the TV series – is no excuse.

In what is claimed to be 'Division One', we see 'Cambridge 0–1 Lincoln'. Neither side has ever been in the top flight. But it gets worse, and not just because the likes of Gosport Borough, 'Croydon T', Worcester and 'Acton T' are listed in Division One. A club called simply 'Manchester' lose 1–4 away at Leicester, but most egregious of all is 'Carlisle T', who lost away at Ipswich. Carlisle T? Carlisle Town? Carlisle became a city in 1133. A disgrace.

JONATHAN WILSON

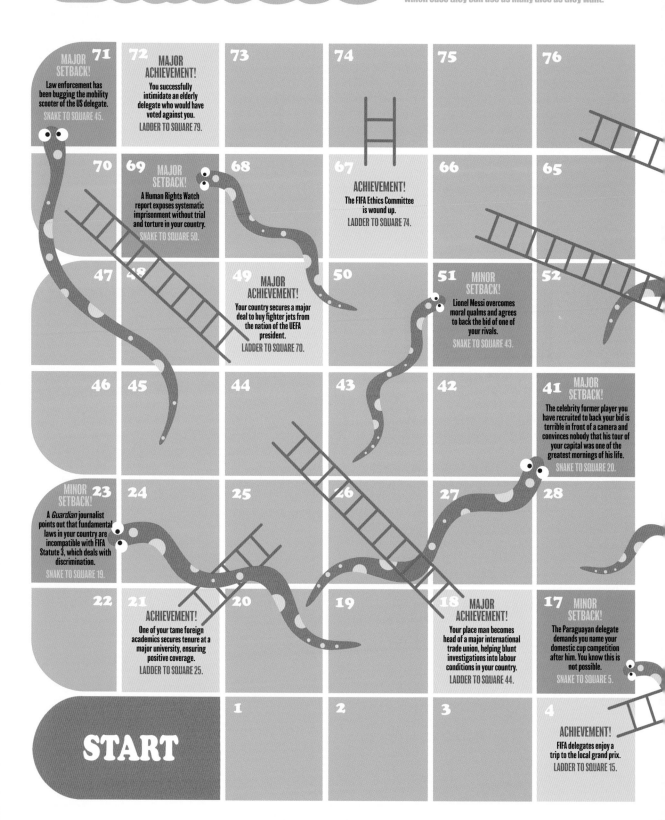

Snakes & Blatters

Can you lead your country's bid through the viper's nest of FIFA politics to earn the right to host the next World Cup?

Each player should select a country to represent and use a coin as a counter, unless representing a petrostate, in which case a gold ingot or barrel of oil should be used instead. Players should roll one die per turn, unless they are representing a petrostate, in which case they can use as many dice as they want.

71 MAJOR SETBACK!
Law enforcement has been bugging the mobility scooter of the US delegate.
SNAKE TO SQUARE 45.

72 MAJOR ACHIEVEMENT!
You successfully intimidate an elderly delegate who would have voted against you.
LADDER TO SQUARE 79.

73

74

75

76

70

69 MAJOR SETBACK!
A Human Rights Watch report exposes systematic imprisonment without trial and torture in your country.
SNAKE TO SQUARE 50.

68

67 ACHIEVEMENT!
The FIFA Ethics Committee is wound up.
LADDER TO SQUARE 74.

66

65

47

48

49 MAJOR ACHIEVEMENT!
Your country secures a major deal to buy fighter jets from the nation of the UEFA president.
LADDER TO SQUARE 70.

50

51 MINOR SETBACK!
Lionel Messi overcomes moral qualms and agrees to back the bid of one of your rivals.
SNAKE TO SQUARE 43.

52

46

45

44

43

42

41 MAJOR SETBACK!
The celebrity former player you have recruited to back your bid is terrible in front of a camera and convinces nobody that his tour of your capital was one of the greatest mornings of his life.
SNAKE TO SQUARE 20.

23 MINOR SETBACK!
A *Guardian* journalist points out that fundamental laws in your country are incompatible with FIFA Statute 3, which deals with discrimination.
SNAKE TO SQUARE 19.

24

25

26

27

28

22

21 ACHIEVEMENT!
One of your tame foreign academics secures tenure at a major university, ensuring positive coverage.
LADDER TO SQUARE 25.

20

19

18 MAJOR ACHIEVEMENT!
Your place man becomes head of a major international trade union, helping blunt investigations into labour conditions in your country.
LADDER TO SQUARE 44.

17 MINOR SETBACK!
The Paraguayan delegate demands you name your domestic cup competition after him. You know this is not possible.
SNAKE TO SQUARE 5.

START

1

2

3

4 ACHIEVEMENT!
FIFA delegates enjoy a trip to the local grand prix.
LADDER TO SQUARE 15.

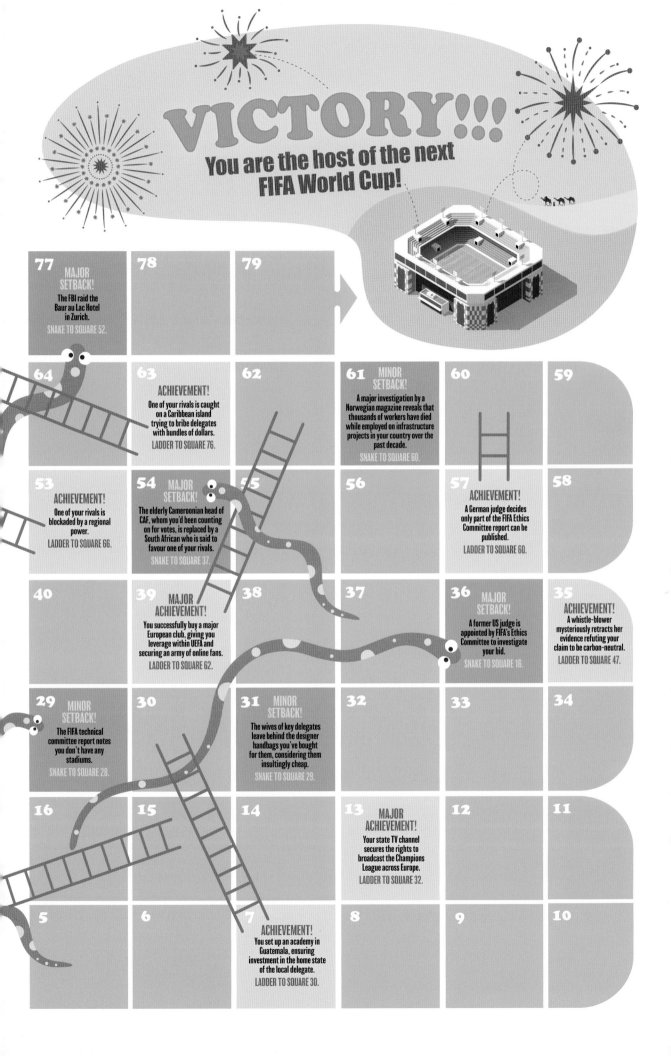

VICTORY!!!

You are the host of the next FIFA World Cup!

77 MAJOR SETBACK!
The FBI raid the Baur au Lac Hotel in Zurich.
SNAKE TO SQUARE 52.

78

79

64

63 ACHIEVEMENT!
One of your rivals is caught on a Caribbean island trying to bribe delegates with bundles of dollars.
LADDER TO SQUARE 76.

62

61 MINOR SETBACK!
A major investigation by a Norwegian magazine reveals that thousands of workers have died while employed on infrastructure projects in your country over the past decade.
SNAKE TO SQUARE 60.

60

59

53 ACHIEVEMENT!
One of your rivals is blockaded by a regional power.
LADDER TO SQUARE 66.

54 MAJOR SETBACK!
The elderly Cameroonian head of CAF, whom you'd been counting on for votes, is replaced by a South African who is said to favour one of your rivals.
SNAKE TO SQUARE 37.

55

56

57 ACHIEVEMENT!
A German judge decides only part of the FIFA Ethics Committee report can be published.
LADDER TO SQUARE 60.

58

40

39 MAJOR ACHIEVEMENT!
You successfully buy a major European club, giving you leverage within UEFA and securing an army of online fans.
LADDER TO SQUARE 62.

38

37

36 MAJOR SETBACK!
A former US judge is appointed by FIFA's Ethics Committee to investigate your bid.
SNAKE TO SQUARE 16.

35 ACHIEVEMENT!
A whistle-blower mysteriously retracts her evidence refuting your claim to be carbon-neutral.
LADDER TO SQUARE 47.

29 MINOR SETBACK!
The FIFA technical committee report notes you don't have any stadiums.
SNAKE TO SQUARE 28.

30

31 MINOR SETBACK!
The wives of key delegates leave behind the designer handbags you've bought for them, considering them insultingly cheap.
SNAKE TO SQUARE 29.

32

33

34

16

15

14

13 MAJOR ACHIEVEMENT!
Your state TV channel secures the rights to broadcast the Champions League across Europe.
LADDER TO SQUARE 32.

12

11

5

6

7 ACHIEVEMENT!
You set up an academy in Guatemala, ensuring investment in the home state of the local delegate.
LADDER TO SQUARE 30.

8

9

10

Right, finally, what we've all been looking forward to. Nobody going to interrupt? No silliness about microwaves or U-Bahns? Anybody? Max? Barry? No? Great. So at last we can get on with the real business: content based on Austro-Hungarian football from the first half of the twentieth century.

The grid below contains the names of twenty-five great Hungarian coaches. When you've found all their names, enjoy the secret message hidden in the rest of the grid.

HUNGARIAN WORD SEARCH

```
P E L E A S R E S S O L H C S E
B I U Y M Y B A O O I K A B O U
S S Z T E I D T N H U V N G A R
C E I A N F K A H L O O O T B A
H N L L T B E I R E O T R K N M
A H W E E O R N N A M T T U G
F O W O R S T L D I O W H L A B
F F G A C R E H O E N K B E R A
E F A H N D S T H T E U U N B P
R E L Z I E Z C R S I R S N I N
G R L I T T O S E B E S O A K L
O P O Z S O N Y I R A C D M S O
F R W E S E A R C E H H A D A N
D I I S O R A S T H W N I L N K
I T C S Y S S E Y G D E M E G E
N U H I N E L Y G I R R E F A T
```

Blum	Eisenhoffer	Hirschl	Medgyessy	Schaffer
Braun	Erbstein	Kertesz	Molnar	Schlosser
Bukovi	Feldmann	Konrad	Orth	Sebes
Czeizler	Gallowich	Kurschner	Pozsonyi	Toth
Dietz	Guttmann	Mandi	Sarosi	Weisz

Full name: Barry John Glendenning
Birthplace: Portiuncla Hospital, Ireland
Previous/other clubs/media outlets: Birr Town FC, Birr GAA club, Birr RFC, *Hot Press*, talkSPORT

BARRY GLENDENNING

Job or trade before becoming a journalist: General dogsbody and lackey in a rural Irish veterinary practice, petrol-pump attendant, waiter
Favourite player: The pre-pandemic Matt Le Tissier
Favourite other podcast: *The Socially Distant Sports Bar*
Childhood football hero: Kenny Dalglish
Favourite other sports: Hurling, rugby, horse racing, snooker, cricket
Other sportsperson you most admire: Rory McIlroy
Most memorable match: Offaly 3–16, Limerick 2–13, All-Ireland Hurling Final, 1994. The mother of all comebacks in what is now known as 'the five-minute final'
Best stadium visited: There is no finer sporting cathedral than Croke Park on All-Ireland Final day
Favourite food and drink: Ribeye steak, salad and chips; Guinness, coffee, Coke Zero
Miscellaneous likes: Pubs
Miscellaneous dislikes: Pub bores, even though I probably am one
Favourite music: A lot of Britpop stuff recorded before 1999
Favourite actor: Colm Meaney
Best film seen recently: I never, ever tire of watching *Raiders of the Lost Ark*
Favourite activity on day off: A long walk followed by an afternoon in my local pub
Biggest influence on career: Irish journalist Liam Mackey, who mentored me at *Hot Press*, and the wishy-washy, leftie broadcaster Max Rushden, who unwittingly mentors me on a daily basis
Superstitions: I always greet and salute solitary magpies
International honours: Fastest walker on last year's *Guardian Football Weekly* tour of the UK and Ireland. The rest of them don't half dawdle from hotel to venue to nearby pub
Personal ambition: I am largely content and have no ambition whatsoever
Which person in the world would you most like to meet? Somewhat incredibly, I have realised my ambition of meeting Kylie Minogue. It was in a backstreet Dublin pub. She was with Michael Hutchence. I mistook them for a couple of Aussie backpackers and gave them tourist advice

Full name: Max Paul Rushden
Birthplace: Cambridge, England
Car: A Suburu something. My first car was a Y-reg Clio. I sold it on Darren Eadie's 'Sellebrity' charity website. Valued at £1,000; added my celebrity name to it, and it sold for £600

MAX RUSHDEN

Previous/other clubs/media outlets: Hills Road Is 1995–7, Oxford University IIIs 1998–2001, Keble College Is 1998–2001, XMVC Dolphins 2001–3, Polytechnic IVs 2003–present (still registered), University of Melbourne Bohemians 2022–present
Job or trade before becoming a journalist: Punt chauffeur, receptionist
Favourite player: Wes Hoolahan
A player for the future: Luka Modrić – not tired yet
Favourite other podcast: *Football Clichés*, *Newscast*
Childhood football hero: Michael Cheetham, Teddy Sheringham, Glenn Hoddle
Favourite other sports: Cricket, golf
All-time favourite XI: John Vaughan; Andy Fensome, Danny O'Shea, Phil Chapple, Alan Kimble; Michael Cheetham, Glenn Hoddle, Wes Hoolahan, Lee Philpott; John Taylor, Dion Dublin. Bench: Steve Claridge, Teddy Sheringham, Neville Southall
Most memorable match: Cambridge 0, Cardiff 0. David Elleray sent three of their players off – one for handling it on the line. We missed the penalty
Biggest disappointment: Not being at St James' Park for Newcastle 0, Cambridge 1 in the FA Cup last year.
Best stadium visited: San Siro
Favourite food and drink: Any classic pasta in any trattoria in Italy. A pint of bitter in an old-man pub in the UK in winter – can't get a good bitter in Australia
Miscellaneous likes: A side-foot pass, stanchions, the 1990s, Scrabble, my porch and Amiga football games
Miscellaneous dislikes: Poppers on baby clothes, reaching under the pram to try and find something, especially while moving, erecting baby furniture with an Allen key, players who refuse to play the way they're facing, lane swimming, marking players at corners, F1, drinking shots, noisy places, ageing, presenters who are rude to producers
Favourite music: *Now That's What I Call Music!* 12–26
Favourite actor: Alan Fletcher
Best film seen recently: *Robin Hood: Prince of Thieves*.
Favourite TV show: *Curb Your Enthusiasm*; pretty much any one-hour detective show
Favourite activity on day off: Morning coffee with Mrs Rushden, playing football
Personal ambition: Rinse the Australian youth sporting set-up so that baby Ian Rush(den) opens the batting for England despite having the broadest Aussie accent
If not a journalist, what would you do? Be a bad lawyer

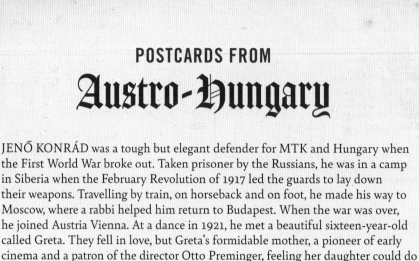

POSTCARDS FROM
Austro-Hungary

JENŐ KONRÁD was a tough but elegant defender for MTK and Hungary when the First World War broke out. Taken prisoner by the Russians, he was in a camp in Siberia when the February Revolution of 1917 led the guards to lay down their weapons. Travelling by train, on horseback and on foot, he made his way to Moscow, where a rabbi helped him return to Budapest. When the war was over, he joined Austria Vienna. At a dance in 1921, he met a beautiful sixteen-year-old called Greta. They fell in love, but Greta's formidable mother, a pioneer of early cinema and a patron of the director Otto Preminger, feeling her daughter could do better than a footballer eleven years her senior, sent Greta to stay with her uncle in Berlin. When she found out that Greta had danced at a club with a woman dressed as a man, though, she brought her home and accepted the marriage to Konrád. He pursued a successful managerial career throughout the 1930s, before the Nazi advance forced the family to flee. They eventually escaped to the US on a boat exporting cork from Lisbon.

◆———◆———◆

HUNGARY WERE so humiliated by losing 3–0 to Egypt at the 1924 Paris Olympics that a parliamentary inquiry was established to find out what had gone wrong. The players gave their testimony, which was collected in what became known as the 'Black Book'. Some blamed petty rivalries; others blamed the food – the forward Csibi Braun spoke of meagre breakfasts of 'coffee and bread and butter' and 'half-raw bloody meat for lunch', which perhaps says less about its quality than its Frenchness. But everybody agreed that the Hotel Haussmann in Montmartre, apparently chosen because it facilitated the socialising of delegates, had been a disaster. The centre-half Béla Guttmann reported that the Fogl brothers, who formed the heart of the defence, 'could not sleep but instead caught a dreadfully huge rat, which they nailed to the doorpost'.

◆———◆———◆

JÓZSEF TURAY would become one of the outstanding forwards of the Hungarian game in the inter-war years, his smouldering looks making him a major star. But in 1926, aged twenty-one, he was still just a hopeful, looking for a chance. The manager of MTK, Gyula Feldmann, invited him for a trial and told him to come

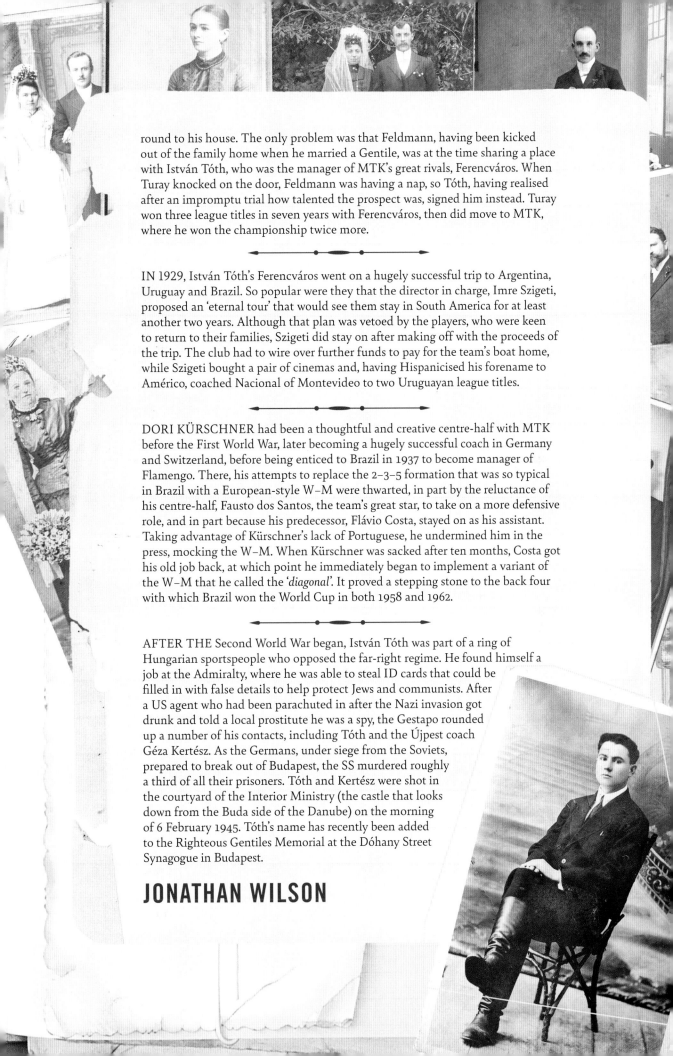

round to his house. The only problem was that Feldmann, having been kicked out of the family home when he married a Gentile, was at the time sharing a place with István Tóth, who was the manager of MTK's great rivals, Ferencváros. When Turay knocked on the door, Feldmann was having a nap, so Tóth, having realised after an impromptu trial how talented the prospect was, signed him instead. Turay won three league titles in seven years with Ferencváros, then did move to MTK, where he won the championship twice more.

IN 1929, István Tóth's Ferencváros went on a hugely successful trip to Argentina, Uruguay and Brazil. So popular were they that the director in charge, Imre Szigeti, proposed an 'eternal tour' that would see them stay in South America for at least another two years. Although that plan was vetoed by the players, who were keen to return to their families, Szigeti did stay on after making off with the proceeds of the trip. The club had to wire over further funds to pay for the team's boat home, while Szigeti bought a pair of cinemas and, having Hispanicised his forename to Américo, coached Nacional of Montevideo to two Uruguayan league titles.

DORI KÜRSCHNER had been a thoughtful and creative centre-half with MTK before the First World War, later becoming a hugely successful coach in Germany and Switzerland, before being enticed to Brazil in 1937 to become manager of Flamengo. There, his attempts to replace the 2–3–5 formation that was so typical in Brazil with a European-style W–M were thwarted, in part by the reluctance of his centre-half, Fausto dos Santos, the team's great star, to take on a more defensive role, and in part because his predecessor, Flávio Costa, stayed on as his assistant. Taking advantage of Kürschner's lack of Portuguese, he undermined him in the press, mocking the W–M. When Kürschner was sacked after ten months, Costa got his old job back, at which point he immediately began to implement a variant of the W–M that he called the '*diagonal*'. It proved a stepping stone to the back four with which Brazil won the World Cup in both 1958 and 1962.

AFTER THE Second World War began, István Tóth was part of a ring of Hungarian sportspeople who opposed the far-right regime. He found himself a job at the Admiralty, where he was able to steal ID cards that could be filled in with false details to help protect Jews and communists. After a US agent who had been parachuted in after the Nazi invasion got drunk and told a local prostitute he was a spy, the Gestapo rounded up a number of his contacts, including Tóth and the Újpest coach Géza Kertész. As the Germans, under siege from the Soviets, prepared to break out of Budapest, the SS murdered roughly a third of all their prisoners. Tóth and Kertész were shot in the courtyard of the Interior Ministry (the castle that looks down from the Buda side of the Danube) on the morning of 6 February 1945. Tóth's name has recently been added to the Righteous Gentiles Memorial at the Dóhany Street Synagogue in Budapest.

JONATHAN WILSON

CLASSIFIEDS

FOR SALE

FRISK'S WHISKS

Stainless Steel & Silicone Non-Stick Coated Small Whisk Set 8" 10" 12" Kitchen Whisk Wire Whisks for Cooking 3 Pack, Black. £15.99.

★★★★ TIM ROBBINS DVDS ★★★★
The Peter Hucker Proxy.
Luke Shaw's Shank Redemption.
Max Gradel Will Rock. Prêt-à-Gary Porter.

SQUIRREL, not living. A Knill, Scunthorpe.

ONE FOREHEAD, BARELY USED.
T Brooking, West Ham.

SAND. Lots of it. Ideal for pitch corners. J Beck, Cambridge.

★ **BOTTLE OF SALAD CREAM** ★
Lid missing. D Beasant, 1994.

DURKIN'S GHERKINS

PICKLED FROM FRESH
Selected for size and pickled soon after picking to retain their crunch.
BONUS OFFER:
Add Elleray's Celeries, Orsato's Tomatoes and Makkelie's Broccolis for the full salad experience.

TAYLOR'S OF WATFORD ENTRANCE SOLUTIONS
Add character to your door with our wide selection of doorbells in traditional and modern styles. 'Can we not knock it?'

GARAGE-STORED VINTAGE HAMS. S Lowe. Madrid.

★★★★ TOM CRUISE DVDS ★★★★
Reina man. Top Bunn. Eyes Carl Shutt.
Days of Cengiz Ünder. Harry Maguire.
Sarr and Mané. The Last Januzaj.

CANN'S CANS!
NEED A CAN?
DARREN CANN

★★★★ COLIN FIRTH DVDS ★★★★
Graham Taylor, Soldier, Spy. Phil King's Speech.
Relative Kalous. Craig Shakespeare in Love.
McBride and Prejudice. Vinnie Jones's Diary.

GOLF CLUBS
One Driver. Used once. Slight dent. £99 ono.
C Bellamy, Wales.
Multiple wedges. Used frequently, still exquisite.
D Bergkamp, Amsterdam.

COMFY CHAIR
Never sat in. £200. J Humphrey, Norfolk.
★★★★★★★★★★★★★★★★★★★

MEIER'S TYRES

SWISS-ENGINEERED FOR A FIRMER GRIP

JULIA ROBERTS DVDS
Pretty Coman.
Sleeping with McMenemy.
Beattie, Pelé, Ndlovu.
Callum Wilson's War.
Klose.

WHIMSICAL METAPHORS
5 for £10. Contact B Ronay, Lewisham.

ONE RED CARD. UNUSED.
Karl-Josef Assenmacher, referee, Netherlands v England 1993, Hürth, Germany.

ONE RED CARD. UNUSED.
Charles Corver, referee, World Cup semi-final 1982, Leiden, Netherlands.

ONE RED CARD. UNUSED.
Howard Webb, referee, World Cup final 2014, Rotherham, South Yorkshire.

First published by Guardian Faber in 2023
Guardian Faber is an imprint of Faber & Faber Ltd,
The Bindery, 51 Hatton Garden
London EC1N 8HN

Guardian is a registered trade mark of
Guardian News & Media Ltd,
Kings Place, 90 York Way, London N1 9GU

Designed and typeset by Ghost Design
Printed and bound in Italy by Printer Trento Srl

The right of Jonathan Wilson, Max Rushden and Barry Glendenning to
be identified as editors of this work has been asserted in accordance with
Section 77 of the Copyright, Designs and Patents Act 1988

A CIP record for this book
is available from the British Library

ISBN 978-1-78335-290-6

10 9 8 7 6 5 4 3 2 1

MIX
Paper | Supporting
responsible forestry
FSC® C015829